Uncommon Entrance

From being awkward on the land during the war Edward Blishen turned after it to being awkward as a teacher (wonderfully unqualified) in a London prep school. *Uncommon Entrance* brings to the richly odd world of high-flying private education the astonished and attentive eye of an apprentice schoolmaster who came from a totally different background. Which was true also of the love affair he had, back home in Barton-on-the-Hill, with Rose-M: who lived at 'the leafy end of town', where houses had names, telephones abounded and Rose-M's terrifyingly skittish mother wore spectacles that were 'not so much an aid to vision as a work of art propped on an unusual easel.'

This is a story full of social, sexual and educational amazement, and of wry delight as gaucheries and disasters are recalled. It is also a gloss on the terrible liveliness of small boys ('Something horribly like actual drunkenness now possessed my little charges'), on the beautiful oddity of their budding characters, and on the nature of the professional prep school teacher, from Mr Juniper, who ran the school on the basis of sudden impatient ideas, some dismaying in their effect, to Mr Hollow, who taught mathematics (and required boys to attend extra lessons in that subject) by means of a careful unintelligibility.

EDWARD BLISHEN

Uncommon Entrance

HAMISH HAMILTON
LONDON

TO THE MEMORY OF
SPENCER VAUGHAN-THOMAS,
with a lifetime's gratitude

First published in Great Britain 1974
by Thames & Hudson Ltd
First published in this edition 1983
by Hamish Hamilton Ltd
Garden House 57–59 Long Acre London WC2E 9JZ

Copyright © Edward Blishen 1974

ISBN 0–241–10920–5

Printed and bound in Great Britain by
Redwood Burn Ltd, Trowbridge, Wiltshire

Contents

PART ONE
page 7

PART TWO
page 67

PART THREE
page 101

Author's Note

Memoirs normally are (or attempt to be) judicious, sober, exact. These are not memoirs of that kind. The worlds of private education, social confusion and blundering love are not fabrications of mine; and certainly I have not conjured up from my imagination the dreadful winter of 1946-47. But I have (to use an interesting current term) re-cycled my memories. In pursuit of truth to experience rather than truth to fact, I have shaped the resulting pulp into people, places and episodes that are inventions entirely.

Part One

I

The Vale, I'd gathered, was a pretty important school. The headmaster had referred to this quality himself, in a letter. 'Mr Bassett has spoken of you very warmly. I can make no promises, of course. We have many distinguished parents and they expect much of The Vale. But come along and let us have a chat.'

This Mr Bassett was an acquaintance of the father of a friend – a bank manager. I barely knew him, but understood that he was a great shaper of other men's lives. My friend had counselled me to avoid him. 'He's interested in you – because he's heard that you read books, and write poems, and all that. And when he's interested in people, he wants to . . . push them around . . . mould their destinies. Don't let him get his hands on you. He can be horribly persistent.'

But I'd run into Mr Bassett in our local High Street. He'd asked me at once what I meant to do now the war was over. 'A young fellow like you should feel many tugs.' It sounded maritime, I thought. I saw myself being swung round in mid-channel, my funnels furiously smoking. . . . 'You say you've thought of going back to local newspaper reporting. Do you feel that this would lead to the full use of your skills?' The tugs swung me round violently, pointing my bows now this way, now that. 'You say many people must have flirted with the idea of teaching. It seems to me an idea a young fellow like you should . . . rather more than flirt with.' I saw Rose-M passing on the other side of the road, in the company of that curious parody of her, her mother. I struggled to slip from the control of my tugs. I let off several shrill blasts of my . . . What the devil did they call that whistle thing up on the funnel? Oh, a whistle, of course. 'I shall certainly speak to the headmaster of The Vale. They bank with us. He spoke when I last saw him of a vacancy.'

I thought no more of it. The Vale was a prep school. That was a world I didn't belong to, and indeed was opposed to on the most insistent grounds of principle. Nine years before I had failed Higher School Certificate after a stormy career in the grammar school sixth form: if I *was* a ship, then academically I had been most fantastically holed. Reading, writing and amateur acting had given me this air attractive to a benevolent busybody like Mr Bassett. But it was all right – I was safe from The Vale. Well, take James.

James was the friend whose father was diffidently acquainted with Mr Bassett. James and I had won the scholarship together from the elementary school, we'd gone to the grammar school together. James was a regular, and of late a dreaded, visitor to my home. He imagined himself a musician, and would use our piano to feed this fantasy. There'd been a recent evening when he pushed past me as soon as I opened the front door and made his way into the room we called the drawing room. There, he seated himself at the piano. 'I've been trying out *Elijah*,' he mumbled; then placed a foot on the loud pedal, muttered to himself, and held his hands, arched for octaves or worse, over the extremities of the keyboard. They bounced down: an awful thunder of inaccuracy filled the room.

It was a small house. My parents were in the living room, a thin wall away.

James muttered again and looked at me over his shoulder unseeingly. Then he felt once more in the air with arched hands, as though the important thing in playing the piano was to place the hands in a correct preparatory position well clear of it; again they bounced down, and now they began to skid this way and that, to hesitate, to commit new inaccuracies in the attempt to amend old ones.

And all the time the loud pedal was down, so that none of these appalling sounds disappeared: layer after layer of wrong notes hung in the air. Then James began to sing.

I could hear my parents stirring amazedly, next door.

James had a natural bass voice but always preferred to assume an unnatural one, hideously profound. The room shook with it all. The framed photographs danced on the piano lid. Then James looked again at me, sightless, biting his lips. He turned side on to the piano, as though at all costs he must not see it, and scrabbled diabolically in the bass. His voice unbelievably sank lower.

'I say . . .' I protested.

But already my mother had rushed into the room. 'No, no . . .!' she was crying. James happened to be looking in her direction and he gave her a little nod. 'No! No!' she cried again. James repeated his nod. He was nibbling now at his lip frantically, and his hands were approaching the upper reaches of the keyboard with a screwing motion, as though they meant to *wring* music from the instrument. 'No!' my mother shrieked: whereupon James hesitated and said, 'Mmmm?' 'That's too noisy,' panted my mother. 'Eh?' said James.

My father appeared in the doorway, holding a napkin to his lips. 'My God,' he said, 'what is this?' 'My husband doesn't like it,' said

8

my mother hotly. 'I mean,' said my father, 'it sounded like the end of the whole bloody world . . .'

No friend of James, surely, was in danger of being offered a post at The Vale . . .

I wasn't sure what effect Rose-M might have on my prospects. I'd met her, not long before, in the ranks of a local discussion group. This was called The Under Thirties. It was James who had dragged me into it, on the grounds that it would sharpen our wits. 'My mind,' James declared, 'has been blunted by my years in the RAF.' I'd stared at him wildly when he said this: partly because I could never really believe that James had spent the war with the Air Force. My old school friend had a profoundly domestic and undramatic nature: so much so that I couldn't understand how, once James had enlisted, the RAF had continued with such hazardous activities as flying aeroplanes. James had himself methodically stuck to the ground, a clerk. At one point he'd been sent to India. From that amazing continent had come letters carefully recording the local temperatures, local prices: the height of a hill climbed, the date of a temple visited. James had made India seem an extension of our local High Street.

So I was always surprised by James's references to those years; and on this occasion I was further startled by his claim to have had his mind blunted by the RAF. The beauty of James's mind, ever since I'd first known him as a child of six or seven, had been its bluntness. In fact, a little thought told me that James had joined The Under Thirties in the hope of meeting girls. It was another difference between us, emerging from the long identity of our fates as schoolboys and then as victims of the war, which had swallowed the years between our late teens and our mid-twenties. I was terrified of actual women, and endlessly hopeful in respect of a phantasmal woman planted in my head by long years of chaste speculation and passionate imagination. James, on the other hand, was brisk and forward in sexual matters, but thoroughly matter-of-fact. He went to places in order to meet girls. Having met them, he had with the assenting ones what, with some archness, he called 'affairs'. 'I'm having an affair with a little dark girl called Daphne.' 'Five foot four and three-quarter inches tall?' I would hazard. 'Takes size 9 in stockings?' 'Size 8,' James might say. 'And you're a quarter of an inch out in her height.'

He had led me to believe that The Under Thirties might be a vividly radical group. They would discuss the great diseases of the post-war world in the spirit of surgeons: they would lean towards severe remedies. But I was disappointed. Once a week we met to listen to a talk about local history: about Famous London Taverns – most of them destroyed in the blitz, we were informed by an amazingly thirsty-looking lecturer: about The Techniques of the Lithographer. I felt I hadn't survived those years of bellicose boredom in order to taste such peaceable tediums as these. And indeed I should have left the group if it had not been for Rose-M.

Rose-M had joined The Under Thirties out of expectations precisely opposite to my own. She had long since decided that all the evils in the world sprang from the incautious confession of opinion. Say you believed something, and at once someone else sprang up to say he was opposed to your belief. Result, misery: at best, noisy behaviour. Given command of things, Rose-M would have forbidden the statement of all attitudes, outlooks, views. The Under Thirties had been recommended to her as a group that offered amiable companionship most innocuously weighted with lectures. When I got to know her well, I understood that, to Rose-M, the word 'lecture' must have been one of the most disarming of all words. She believed that, in its very nature, a lecture must be concerned with unworldly topics, free of all harm and controversy. 'I thought it would be about Persian pottery,' she once told me generally. She, too, was disappointed. She had not bargained for the question times that followed the lectures. These, even when it was some far-off matter of local history, sometimes produced moments of waspish dissension – as to a date, a name. James was often responsible: he could be quite menacing when roused to defend a fact. Rose-M feared that she'd blundered into some revolutionary cell.

But she'd also blundered into me. Among the amazing promises that the return of peace seemed capable of offering was that some attractive girl would turn out to be the woman in my head. *She*, briefly, was an incredibly beautiful bluestocking, at one and the same time all heart and all brain. Her looks combined ice and fire. Rose-M was a pretty child, but wrought of elements less drastic than these. She was not a bluestocking at all. Had one to invent a term for her along those lines, it would be . . . palest pink stocking with silver stars, perhaps. But my very clear knowledge of these discrepancies, between ideal and reality, lasted barely beyond our first meeting. There was a moment when I was quite consciously despairing of her name. Rosemary Perkins, she was called. It was no name for the sort of woman I had in mind. I thought her nose too sharp, her cheekbones too prominent. Then she caught me in a corner of the room. She'd heard of me, she said, from a friend of the family – her father's bank manager, in fact: a Mr Bassett. He had spoken glowingly of me. Her hand lay on my arm as she said this, very lightly. Her friends, by the way, called her Rose-M. I was interested, she'd heard, in music: it was one of *her* warmest interests, too. It was nice, wasn't it, to think we both . . .

She went away from that first meeting with a girl friend, waving at me from the door. I walked home with James, addressing at him a remark or two about pretty girls with empty heads who occupied one's time with polite banalities. James retorted with praise, largely statistical, of her bosom and bottom. 'My dear James,' I said. 'Your next affair, I fancy . . .'

I woke the next morning shaking with terror: would my honest, prosaic friend dare to lay this delicate creature under his dull spell? I thought of the sensitive shape of her nose, of the lovely triangle made by her chin and those strange cheekbones. Her name spoke itself in my head, over and over, a great enchantment. Rosemary Perkins. I liked the way the romantic mistiness of the first name was crossed by the brisk good sense of the second. And if I unhooked that second and replaced it with my own, the effect remained agreeably similar.

To our second meeting I went with great excitement, interrupted by short growling lectures addressed at myself: 'facile fixation' was a prominent phrase in these, before they gave way to dizzy dreams – and sudden despairs: she hated me, of course, had reason to know that my love of music was based on shaky judgments . . . Mr Bassett was a friend of her family. My family included among its friends no one half so elevated as a bank manager. Oh, she was middle class, of course – they had their friends to *dinner*: candles, wine . . . *napery*. Napery – that was it. What part in my own world was played by *napery*?

I was aloof that second evening, avoided her eye, averted my carefully shaven face. 'You seem far away tonight,' she said, suddenly beside me, her hand on my arm. 'Mysterious. Brooding on something. Walk home with me and tell me what it is.'

I was in the trap, and couldn't imagine being anywhere else. I was in heaven, I was in hell. I listened to her talk, of her wartime experience as a WAAF: her broken education – this convent and that convent, it seemed ('I was a difficult child'). I made such answers as I could to her inquiries. Did I have a favourite pub in the town? And then, when my face twisted with the impossibility of answering – how say that I'd always associated the pubs with the local hearties, the rugby footballers and their friends, all those I'd got on ill with at school? – as I wrestled with this vast tissue of priggishness and social awkwardness, she touched my arm: 'I shouldn't have asked. I can't see you leaning on the bar. Oh, you're so sensitive. It's hard luck on me. You see—' And *that* remark, like so many, uncompleted. Oh, she perfected her capture of me with incomplete remarks! 'I had rather a . . . an emotional time in the WAAF. I was rather – oh well —' 'Perhaps you've heard about the time I was expelled from the convent. Most people in town seem to know about it. Never mind—'

I was hopelessly in love with her; she was the hub of my life: I despised her for her conventionality, her middle classness. I desired her and wished to run from her. And then I met her with her mother. In some disturbing fashion, Mrs. Perkins seemed to be Rose-M thirty years on.

'Oh mummy, this is Edward. I've told you about him. Edward's going to come and listen to music with me.'

'That would be so amusing. Poor Rose-M – so cross with her mummy because we don't *absolutely* agree about music. Do we, darling? Tell me, Edward – are you a Rachmaninoff man?'

That was the point we'd reached – on my part, such passionate attraction, such violent revulsion – when the letter came from Mr Juniper, the headmaster of The Vale, proposing an interview.

From my own outer suburb I went to that inner one, where the poets lived and the clever and beautiful foreigners. The Vale was at the heart of it: two buildings side by side, the junior school and the senior school, among the tall houses that, on that summer evening, seemed husky with voices from Central Europe. You couldn't enter those houses, so high and chastely grey, without mounting the steps that led to their columned porches. So different, I thought in a troubled way, from the simple access to the simple semi-detached I lived in: columnless, pebble-dashed. Oh, I was out of my world again: no doubt about that. I need have no fear. Mr Juniper would see at once that I didn't belong.

He was white-haired, brisk yet absent-minded. He had forgotten I was coming, but somehow was business-like about this. 'I forget rather easily,' he said, and it sounded like an assertion of soundness. 'The Vale is a great responsibility. It's an important school, and much is expected of it.'

'Yes,' I said.

'Tell me about yourself,' he went on. 'You've been a conscientious objector? Recently released from work on the land?'

'Yes,' I said, feeling comfortable. It was going to be a quick review of the many obvious reasons why I should on no account be appointed to the teaching staff of The Vale. 'You've had no previous experience at all? You went to . . . ah yes. I don't know the school. A good school, is it? . . . Mr Bassett tells me you're very interested in literature. I suppose you read – W. H. Auden, T. S. Eliot, and so on?'

I said that was what I did.

'Ah,' he sighed. 'Tell me about W. H. Auden.'

I set out the reasons why W. H. Auden might well be considered for this post. 'Yes,' said Mr Juniper. 'Well – you're young. I mean, you're obviously very fit?'

I thought he meant this followed, perhaps surprisingly, from being a reader of W. H. Auden's poetry. But I assented. 'You wouldn't,' said the headmaster with sudden sharpness, 'feel unable to give a hand with . . . cubbing?'

The question was totally unexpected, and I said hurriedly: 'Oh no, of course.'

The headmaster looked me up and down, as he had already done several times. I was wearing a baggy cheap suit. I thought: 'They'd never have a teacher here wearing a suit like this.' My feeling of the unreality of the interview became sharper: and was crowned when Mr Juniper shook my hand and said, 'You have a telephone number – if I want to get in touch?' I had to say No. We had no telephone at home: had never had one. I was sensitive about that, of late: Rose-M's family had two telephones, and one was beside her mother's bed. I knew there was an absolute unlikelihood that I could be accepted by marriage, or in any other important fashion, into the home of a girl with two telephones.

'Then I'll write and tell you – one way or the other,' said the head-master, becoming absent-minded again. He stared at me without recognition, and looked up and down the swollen lines of my suit with what I thought to be a mixture of hatred and disbelief. He saw me to the main door of the school, as though anxious to be certain that I left the building: and I went with a feeling of slightly sad finality into the famous air of that brilliant suburb. I'd never mount those steps again.

A week later the letter came. It gave the headmaster great pleasure to appoint me to the staff of The Vale. He was certain from our discussion that I had made a proper choice of profession. He wasn't quite sure yet how he might use me. Some work would be in the junior school, and I'd be expected to help with cubbing. Since I was wholly unqualified I would, of course, be regarded as a probationer, and it was understood that I should consider ways of obtaining qualifications. On the same grounds I was being offered a starting salary of £200 a year. I should attend the staff meeting that would take place on the day before the opening of the autumn term, three months away.

'I look forward to having you as a colleague,' was Mr Juniper's final astounding sentence.

2

The thought of becoming a teacher had been a romantic fantasy only: one of several that sprang up as I came to my last days on the land. Stepping out of the prison of war, I'd had the common experience of being dazed by the bright light, the prospect of a free bustle of affairs. One might do anything – become anything. After five and a half years of manual labour, I longed for an occupation of some refined, perhaps rather airless kind, which made it possible to keep one's boots clean. Teaching certainly seemed likely to be such an occupation. The State was running an emergency training scheme, and I toyed with the idea of applying for that. I went beyond toying: I filled in forms. I was told I must wait: the colleges were full. Apply they said, in a year's time.

Odd offshoot of that: here I was, a junior member of the staff of a high-flying prep school. As I understood what had happened, through such a sneaky chain of accidents – that meeting with Mr Bassett, the word he'd dropped in Mr Juniper's ear, the headmaster's own amazing misjudgment – I began to panic, quite profoundly.

Rose-M said: 'Oh, The Vale! Oh, how lovely! I know one or two people who've been there. Including a certain Squadron Leader. Oh well—' Another of her remarks to fade away on a fascinatingly repentant sigh. What sort of life *had* she led? It couldn't have been too wicked, I thought, given the colourful fragility of that face, the plain innocence of the curls at the nape of her neck.

Those curls I'd suddenly become aware of – as if, until then, she'd been perfectly bald. I was constantly making discoveries of this kind. During the first weeks of our acquaintance I'd vaguely thought of her as of considerable height: perhaps about ten feet. One evening I observed precisely that the top of her head was level with my shoulder. I puzzled over the problem of assembling her in my awareness objectively.

'I should think it's just right for you. Such a thoughtful person,' she said.

What was wrong with people? Here was Mr Juniper ignoring the plain sad facts of my record and appointing me to The Vale. Here was Rose-M ignoring facts just as dismaying – among them, my not being a pub-goer, my positively being thoughtful and so a disturber of that unopinionated peace Rose-M was so anxious to secure – and appointing me as . . .

Appointing me to what position vis-à-vis herself?

I had not yet visited her home for that evening of music. 'When will you come?' Rose-M asked whenever we met. At the very hint of so definite a proposal, I flinched away from her. A piece of grit, I snarled in my diary, round which, oyster-like, I was creating a pearl of illusion. She was a *flirt*. 'I am flirting with you, Edward. Do you mind?' 'Oh, is that flirting? If that's what it is, I don't mind.' Oh, my heavy boots, my solemnity, my priggishness! I was angry with her, wasn't I, because I couldn't really be in love with her? There was too much difference of need between us. Oh, it was absurd! She wanted the evening out, drinking, dancing – social chattering. I wanted to talk about – oh! It was all wrong, all wrong. I told my diary, again and again, how wrong it was, and in what particular ways. And each fervently documented description of our incompatibility was followed, at once, by a dream of its being wholly otherwise.

But I couldn't imagine myself in her house, among all those telephones – meeting Mr Perkins, something in industry – listening to music on her gramophone...

'Oh dear, I shan't see you till next week,' she'd sigh.

'That will be nice for you.'

Flippancy, snapped the angry fellow inside me. And hypocrisy, too. Hadn't I, in a recent fulmination in my diary, spoken of her *schoolgirl's jokes*?

She had been admitted to a dancing school. 'Edward, I don't know what has happened to my technique since I joined the WAAF. Mummy says I still have talent, but you know what dancers' mothers are like. But lots of the new girls are in the same boat. Oh, so *distraught*, my dear – wondering if they can pick up their dancing again.'

Distraught! It was Rose-M's favourite word. Mummy was distraught, half the time it seemed, because of tiny refined inconveniences. I was consumed with inward irony. What a brittle child she was!

She smiled at me across a room, and it was not the same Rose-M. A smile of great sweetness. Who *was* Rose-M? How long it took to digest a new acquaintance! Sometimes I seemed to be in the company of another person altogether, not the monster of my private dreads, not the prattling girl, but someone to whose sweetness of expression there seemed to be an immense depth – and I was being drawn into that depth, and was infinitely content to be drawn. This was altogether another girl, with altogether different physical characteristics.

I found myself snatching up the local newspaper when it came on a Friday, and turning to the column of 'Forthcoming Marriages'. She'd be there, I was always sure, she'd be there with Squadron Leader . . . with one of the leading dancers of the . . . with my old friend James . . .

'In a week I shall be going to my friend's farm in Cornwall and then I shall be away for six whole weeks and – Edward, you still haven't come to see us.'

I was preoccupied with my preparations for teaching. But 'preparations' was perhaps hardly the word. I was going to have to teach English: and that presumably meant a good deal of grammar. I'd always had a poor grasp of grammar. There'd been, at school, old Jilly, who'd delighted in working down in the engine-room of language: and had us all down there, for the first two grammar school years, bolting and unbolting the bits and pieces of speech, with Jilly's angers increasing the confusion of his oppressed team of mechanics. I'd never recovered from that. Breaking up sentences was to me as bitter as breaking up stones to a convict. But I'd have to do it at The Vale: so I bought myself a textbook. I would study it. But I didn't. Instead, I sat down day after day and copied out the contents of the textbook, uncomprehendingly. These weren't preparations; they were substitutes for preparation, briefly soothing to the conscience. When I got up from one of those copying sessions, I felt I'd been at work. It was like my feeling that I had come to some stable conclusion about Rose-M. A few hours later, in either case, I'd be attacking myself in my diary.

'By nature, I should say, I am the last person who should become a teacher . . .' 'The dread of being an utter failure, an impostor, an outrageous impostor, is never out of my mind.' 'I have misspent this long holiday. But I must not give way to nightmares.'

I was invited to the junior school to talk to its headmistress. Miss Seakins looked at me with kindly severity. Upper Three, she was certain, would profit immensely from my supervision of their English. She'd like me also to take them for a weekly lesson on the history of London. They were awfully unfamiliar with their own city.

She smiled, and I went away and borrowed from the local library a half a dozen volumes on London. I bought a new notebook and set out on further copyings, abstracts. I sat, making my notes, and was persuaded that I was preparing to be a teacher.

Rose-M went to Cornwall. I celebrated her going with an outburst of irony in my diary. Six weeks on a friend's farm in Cornwall! How could I have hopes in such a direction? People who had friends who had farms were not my people. I imagined her, on horseback with . . . a Squadron Leader in rural mufti . . . I imagined her in infatuated, enchanted taverns on the edge of the Atlantic.

I felt dizzy with love and the recollection of her curls . . .

And the time came for the beginning-of-term staff meeting at The Vale.

On the eve of that meeting I found myself wondering, with sudden distraction, how I could contrive some sort of presentability. In adolescence I'd recoiled altogether from smartness. The argument was simple. To dress neatly was to adopt the style of a slave. The tidy man was saying: 'Look at me, and be assured of my conformity. The cut of my suit is a guarantee of that. My tie is chosen to make clear my freedom from all restive opinion. The shortness of my hair and its cowed character are meant as marks of my meekness.' And so on. The war years had not obliged me to think again about this. It had been a time simply of universal dishevelment. But now . . .

I remembered the way the Head had seemed to be uneasily eyeing my suit, off and on, during our interview. Hadn't there been, in those glances, distaste?

I attacked my hair. Hair oil I wouldn't use. That was a mark of slickness, all right – oiled hair! Ugh! But battering my mop with brushes left it ready to adopt arrangements of its own if stirred by the smallest draught. And such arrangements, surely, were unallowable, gauche.

What sort of censure was I attempting to avoid?

Well, the collars of my shirts! They were bunched and . . . oh, generally foolish, ugly, always, weren't they? Why didn't I know how to tame a collar? My collars proclaimed an ineptitude I now found myself unwilling to expose. And that suit, from the Fifty Shilling Tailors! It was of a thick, brutally rough tweed, not so much thornproof as thorny. How had I ever assented to it, in the shop? It was the colour of unsuccessful marmalade.

My father offered me the use of a suit of his own. This was navy blue, double-breasted – everything I was opposed to, on the loftiest of principles. But now my ideas as to dress were all scattered: I was in the grip of social terror, and didn't know what I thought. All I was certain of was my need of dress that would prevent the Vale staff from gasping with disbelief and displeasure as, for the first time, I entered their company.

My father's suit more than contained me: it left room for more backsides, certainly, an extra torso or two. I looked like some gloomy parcel from which most of the contents had been taken. I tore it off and resumed the tweed, which seemed in the interval to have grown even more vulgarly hairy, more shrilly orange in colour.

For so long, I thought – for so long, *fool*, I had clung to the idea of a romantic and rebellious disorder of dress: and now that, suddenly, neatness seemed necessary, I had neither the knowledge nor the materials to achieve it.

Could I, incidentally, imagine Rose-M riding along the edge of the Atlantic with a man wearing a marmalade suit?

'The new young fellow, eh?' said Mr Diamond, History, one of the senior masters, taking my hand and pumping it with every appearance of scarcely containable delight. ''Normous pleasure! 'Normous pleasure!' He handed me on to another senior, Mr Hollow, Mathematics. Mr Hollow spoke a form of English so beautiful that only an odd consonant or so emerged above its flowing surface. 'Extra sh'der to the wheel! Dam' g'd thing!' he seemed to be saying. These things done, I sat smiling anxiously at the edge of numerous bland conversations.

Extraordinary, the staffroom at The Vale, to someone fresh – but that was not the word – from five years of the humblest sorts of agriculture. On the land we'd gathered round bonfires, seated on logs: there'd been spitting, the telling of stories of an animal simplicity . . . long silences intermitted with belches and grunts . . .

The conversation here was like the sandwiches we were eating: thin, dainty, swiftly digestible. I heard the voice of Mrs Leach, English: it seemed to be leaning back, her voice, away from the world, generally bent on avoidance. 'Personally,' she was saying, 'I believe that direct-method Latin will bring the whole system down about our ears. How *do* you examine what will have become . . . mere chatter?' 'My dear lady!' said Mr Raisin, Classics, from the depths of an arm-chair. To say anything from an armchair so profound was clearly a major physical problem, and Mr Raisin gave up, puffing. 'A fatal surrender to fashion, in my view,' said Mrs Leach, who was accepting a limited amount of support from a cane chair, narrow and upright.

'Gentlemen, gentlemen!' cried Mr Juniper, bustling in with Miss Seakins. 'Let's get started at once, shall we?'

Impatience, I was to discover, was one of Mr Juniper's main char-acteristics. He swept through life in a constant state of being ahead of his own timetable. The world, on the whole, lagged a half an hour behind him. The school had adjusted to this oddity. Masters enjoying a legitimate and negotiated free period were resigned to being swept from it by the rapid passage of Mr Juniper. 'Oh, I say, do go and make yourself busy with some little chaps who are standing about in the garden room,' he'd cry. The garden room was a sort of jumped-up cupboard, abutting on part of The Vale's playground, that boasted some plants in pots. Anyone who dropped through any of the small holes that were constantly opening up in The Vale timetable was sent to the garden room to wait for something to develop. Thus, by sheer accident, Mr Juniper's impatience, coupled with his habit of moving urgently and restlessly through the school, meshed with curious faults in organization, and cured them. This was how much was done at The Vale, through a strange collaboration between one oddity and another.

At the staff meeting, Mr Juniper's first impetuous act was to flip through the pages of a book in which the educational ambitions of all the boys were set out. This boy aimed at Winchester, this at Eton, this at Westminster: a score of other places were mentioned, some of them quite unfamiliar to me. It sounded like a page from one of Shakespeare's histories. Today, it was a matter of emendations, reminders: decisions to be taken as to the aggrandisement or reduction of an ambition.

'Jones F. E. to Charterhouse.'

'Oh never, sir.'

'Absurd, Diamond?'

'Ludicrous, sir. He's Scarforth material at best.'

Some delicate laughter round the table. It seemed that to be material acceptable by Scarforth, wherever that might be, was to fall very low indeed.

'Big head, little in it,' Mr Hollow seemed to exclaim.

'What's brought this up, sir . . . ?'

I didn't understand a word of it. Some of the judgments flying about seemed to me quite ferocious. 'He's a mother's boy, sir!' 'Too meek! Too meek! They'd eat him alive!' 'With respect, sir – he's a thoroughly boring child.' 'My goodness, sir! – not that brainless pudding!'

Feeling so out of place, I began to seize on these phrases as definitions of my probable unsuitability as a master at The Vale. Meek, certainly: boring, possibly. I was not a pudding but I wished I were in possession of some unarguable document in respect of my brains.

Mr Juniper thrust away the important book with a furious cry as he glanced at his watch. 'What are we doing, gentlemen?' He took up a sheaf of papers. Ah yes, he said, there had been a letter from an outraged parent. This man's son had been second in form order but had not received a prize. The boy had felt publicly disgraced; and this seemed a particularly sad result when one considered it might have been avoided by the outlay of five or six shillings. The parent was astounded that The Vale should not have foreseen this. The boy had been, he must repeat, severely traumatized.

'Traumatized, sir?' inquired Mr Diamond.

'That was the word,' said Mr Juniper.

'From the Greek, *trauma*, a wound,' murmured Mr Raisin, Classics.

'*I'll* guarantee to wound him, sir, with a slipper,' grunted Mr Diamond. 'Only give the word.'

'*Atrotos* . . . Unwoundable,' said Mr Raisin. 'The boy, I mean.'

'Exactly,' said Mr Juniper. 'I wondered if I might not write and say that the fellow in question was one of the most—'

'Invulnerable,' proposed Mr Raisin.

'One of the most invulnerable, thank you, Mr Raisin, we have ever tried to—'

'"Vulnerate" is a remote possibility,' murmured Mr Raisin. 'It was in occasional use, I believe, between 1600 and, say, 1750.'

'But I thought he would not see the point,' said Mr Juniper. 'So I wrote informing him that there were . . . other considerations in our minds when we awarded prizes. Other, I mean, than form order. And I made it clear that it was not a matter of five or six shillings.'

'Oh, I should jolly well think not,' exploded Mr Diamond.

'But,' said Mr Juniper, 'I said I was willing to make a special award to the boy by way of any public ceremony his father cared to nominate, if that would heal the – ah – '

'Trauma,' said Mr Diamond, wonderingly.

'Exactly. And I've had no reply.'

'Ha! Well done, Headmaster!'

'It . . . stopped them in their tracks, I fancy.'

'It would! It would!' Mr Diamond collected smiles round the table. 'Well handled, sir!'

We appointed prefects. The candid characterizations here were even more striking than when the boys' hopes of this public school or that were being discussed. One nomination produced a volley of amazed laughter. 'Sly, sir.' 'Been creeping up on the appointment all his school life.' 'Ambition matched only by ineptitude!' '*Extraordinary father!*' 'Missel minor's uncle.' 'Good God, sir, that explains it.' 'The Case of the Missing Swimming Pool Keys, sir.' 'I thought that might linger in someone's memory.' 'Oh, good heavens, sir. There we tiptoed round a scandal!' 'Indeed, indeed!' 'The consensus, then – that's become a fashionable word, by the way – have you noticed, Mrs Leach?' 'Perfectly good Latin, sir. You remember your Cicero – *Omnium consensus naturae vox est* etc?' 'Is anyone going to be able to quote Cicero after a few years of direct-method Latin, Mr Raisin?' 'Oh come, Mrs Leach – ' 'Gentlemen – I can't think why we're so far behind the clock – no accolade for young Pompson, then?'

Mr Juniper came to a matter of misadministration that might have been quite grave in its consequences but for the magnanimity of a member of the staff. He referred to a very curious error by which Lower Five had this term been allowed to be nineteen strong. Yes, he didn't blame his colleagues for whistling between their teeth at that. It was a prodigious burden for anyone and he hadn't looked forward to asking some member of staff to take it on. But Mr Diamond had most kindly volunteered for the task. Other masters, he was sure, would wish to demonstrate their admiration and gratitude by little helpfulnesses. It could be left to them.

There was a murmur of applause and relief round the table.

'Oh, it's nothing,' said Mr Diamond. 'Truly, nothing! A boy here or there has never meant much to me. I have my methods, as I think my colleagues know.'

'Nevertheless . . .' said Mr Juniper. 'And now let's get on, gentlemen – good heavens, let's get on!'

I had lost, by now, much of my sense of being a participant, however junior and silent, in this affair. I was a spectator at a play, listening to dialogue much of which was stimulatingly obscure. I was recalled to a sense of my actual presence by Mr Juniper's utterance of my name. '. . . welcome him,' he was saying. 'Where is he? Isn't he with us this afternoon? Miss Seakins – Mr Diamond – isn't—? Ah, there you are! Behind your shoulder, Mr Beesley. A very modest young man!'

I was going to be made, I thought, the subject of a candid characterization. Where would Mr Juniper, so beautifully indifferent to discretion, set the limits? 'Went to a school I've never heard of. You've never heard of it, any of you, gentlemen. His marmalade suit you will all have been eyeing incredulously. I have it on the best authority that he has lately been lusting after an unlucky young dancer. He—'

I was suddenly aware of the faces turned towards me, the kindly smiles. Mr Juniper's, laced though it was with an anguished sense of passing time, was one of the kindest. I felt, as I rose to my feet and approached Mr Diamond for some indication as to the History lesson he wished me to take with Upper Five on the second day of term – I felt a kind of comfort enveloping my general sense of unease and dismay and foreboding.

Upper Five History, like other things I was to be required to teach at The Vale, was outside Mr Juniper's original proposals as to the use he'd make of my services. I was a handyman, I quickly saw: and there were to be moments of terror when I was certain an approaching headmaster would exclaim: 'Oh, I say, do get down to the garden room and give the little chaps a Greek lesson' – or it would be a lesson in pure maths, in Hebrew, in Einsteinian physics . . .

'Mr Diamond,' I said, 'I'm taking History with Upper Five—'

'So you are! So you are!' Mr Diamond spoke with what could only be described as enormously enthusiastic indifference.

'Twice a week—'

'That's it! Quite right! That's the arrangement!'

'And the first occasion will be the morning after next—'

'So it will! Will it? Ah! First class! Couldn't be better!'

'And I wondered if you could give me some—'

'In the morning, old fellow – eh? First thing in the morning, say? Or at teatime, here in the staff room?'

'But it's—'

'I'm awfully glad, old chap. Splendid arrangement! Ah, Raisin—'

3

My working life at The Vale began with assembly next morning in the senior school.

Round the hall ran a gallery; and here parents stood, observing the scene below. I was amazed, noting an actor whose Macduff I'd much admired: two or three polemicists from whose incendiary writings

I myself had drawn little rations of fire: a famous lady novelist: a marvellously infamous comedian. It seemed improbable, altogether – these celebrated masks, coupled with the consideration that small copies and fusions of the same were down in the hall among us and were soon to receive some of their notions of History, English – and the story of London – from me.

We sang the school song, which explored the idea that life was a long preparation for some final and fatal Common Entrance exam. Those who had done well would be received in the eternal public school above. The ultimate headmaster, unstinting in his praises, would offer them something in the nature of an infinite respite from scholarship. Prowess or simple doggedness in games would be taken into account.

> What we've achieved on the field of sport
> Shall be noted down in the Great Report . . .

The fate of those who failed this exam was not glanced at. They would have trodden, one was left to assume, the primrose path to the everlasting State school.

As we dispersed, my terror was enormous. It seemed to me that I was being sternly scrutinized by those parents, drifting glamorously out of the gallery and into the entrance hall. They paid large sums of money to have their important children prepared, not simply for that distant lethal test we'd been singing about, but for the other one so much more imminent, and probably as crucial. I imagined them turning to one another, dismayed. 'An impostor, if ever we saw one . . .'

It was quite without confidence that I walked into my first class-room. Lower Four: 'Give them dictation,' Mrs Leach had said. They were just up from the juniors. 'As new as you'll be,' I'd been assured by a friendly junior school teacher. 'So they'll be no trouble. If you do find things awkward, read them a story.'

I imagined – to cram a huge error into a nutshell – that teaching was lecturing. The night before I had prepared a brief statement of principles as an introduction to my passage of dictation. I'd had in mind . . . oh, vaguely I'd had in mind a group of diminutive professors, who'd be at ease with the faintly sour cadences of my commentary. 'Obviously, if we want to spell correctly in English, we must bring more to the task than our ears.' They would nod carefully, at that. 'There is a connection between the pauses in our speech and the punctuation in our writing: but it cannot always be trusted.' More nodding – a politely concealed yawn or two. Perhaps it *was* very obvious. But then dictation was surely a device for dealing with errors constantly made? How could I know what were the mistakes common in Lower Four? I was, surely, like a surgeon working out the details of an operation in total ignorance of the patient.

In practice, everything was wrong. The faces, to begin with. They were not professorial, lecture-prone. They expressed amazement as I spoke. There was – I felt, panic-stricken – a mysterious but very definite feeling of unsuitability about those general propositions of mine as to the spelling and pointing of the English language.

My lecture rapidly lost the sour crispness I'd designed for it. The room began to whisper. I hurried into the dictation itself. That was a relief – they looked aggrieved, but were busy. It was done: we stared at one another. I made a complex statement containing the idea that, owing to their incredibly sustained good behaviour, I proposed to read them a story of Rudyard Kipling's. This I had selected from a book on the staffroom shelves. It turned out to be far above their heads. They began again to look amazed. The story was also too long – five or six times too long – for the occasion. The bell went, and they began, loudly, to discuss among themselves the unexpected impenetrability of work in the senior school. I dismissed them; but the effect was of their dismissing me.

Followed another English form: Middle Four. Them it did not strike that my nervously elaborate proposals as to the adjective were typical of senior school work. They talked freely and of other topics altogether. 'How then does one identify an adjective . . . ?' 'Sir! Mr Thing! How's your father?' 'I think I'm going to ask very firmly for—' 'Sir, why isn't Mrs Leach taking us this term?' 'Old Mrs Screecher, rotten old teacher!' 'The real point about the adjective—' 'Sir, let's read our comics!' 'I think I'm going to ask you now to take out your exercise books and—' 'Can't, sir! Can't, Mr Thingy! Old Screecher – Mrs Leach took them away last term, and we haven't had them back.' 'Let's go early, Mr Thing!'

I felt like someone standing in the centre of a raging fire before the discovery of the usefulness, in such a situation, of water. How did you—? What did you—?

It was lunch time. Bells went, boys raced impudently out of and into my presence. We were in the hall, having dinner, my head ached; I was in charge of a table, terrible boys were asking me questions of a personal kind . . . I was helping to distribute dishes. My hands were sticky with gravy. The Head, at the top table, was laughing uproariously at some joke told him by a boy. How could anyone smile, let alone laugh? How could one be at ease ever with a male person of prep school age?

It was after lunch: on waves of the most immense noise I'd ever heard I'd been washed over to the junior school. I was in a hall, and cubs were shouting incredible phrases of salutation. I was assisting with a cub pack. Miss Frome . . . a tall, thin, intensely energetic woman called Miss Frome was announcing games. Mr Blishen would take a game of 'O'Grady Says', in the corner over there, with Blues. Blues were finding the mere existence of Mr Blishen stridently funny. All knowledge of 'O'Grady Says' had passed from my mind. I was rescued by Miss Frome, smiling thinly (' "O'Grady says" when you *do* want them to do it, my dear chap!'). The barrier of my skull, which had kept apart the noise in my head and the noise outside it, was suddenly removed, and the two spheres of din became one.

I was making my way home, and my head was full of a red, sore uproar.

And at once it was the following day.

It was one of the most awful days of my life.

Middle Three was my own form: the top but one class in the junior school, a day later than the seniors in starting its term. We shared – it was all you could say – we shared the same room, before the opening assembly. Fifteen boys, most of them nine years old, inspected the stranger who stood, stamped fatally with diffidence and bewilderment, in the corner by the desk. I didn't understand how you began to deal with the problem represented by their relaxation and air of being casually and perfectly at home. It was as if all the supporting characters in a drama were masters of their lines, while the principal character hadn't even begun to study his part. I panicked, and made facile promises of punishment. 'Now, there's going to be very serious trouble if you don't . . .' They didn't, and I had no idea what forms of serious trouble might be at my command. I was not really capable of inflicting even frivolous trouble. I was lost.

Again, enormous noise, enormous tendency of boys not to be sitting in their desks but to be—

I peeped through the glass panels in the door and across, through other panels, at the class that shared our landing. A sabbatical calm and decency reigned there; you could trace the deferential response, somewhere in the room, to the merest lift of the teacher's finger.

Our classes met on the landing, ready to march downstairs. My own was boiling with hilarity. Miss Frome shushed and tutted and shot deadly glances.

In the bright hall we sat and hurdy-gurdily gay tunes tumbled out of the piano. Ladies made small agreeable jokes and the school responded with small agreeable bursts of laughter. Some extremely tiny boys performed on percussion instruments. Miss Seakins spoke sharply once, and a boy shrank and muttered his humblest apologies. The gaiety grew. I sat glum in the midst of it . . .

A reading lesson with my form. *Stories of the Siege of Troy*. 'Begin reading . . . Burgess, is it?' 'Bigears, miss. I mean, sir.' 'I beg your pardon?' 'His name is Bigears.' The entire form had become an undifferentiated giggle. 'Aga – Aga – Aga – meme – meme – yon!' 'You know better than – *Agamemnon*!' Oh, what a foolish reading book – full of these quenching Greek names. 'Give me my car, you fool!' 'You gave it to me last term!' 'You liar!' 'Put those toy cars away! No, bring them here!' 'What toys, sir?' 'Those you've just put in your pockets – oh, let's have some *silence* while we're reading!' When the poor story had limped to a close, accompanied by irrelevances and increasingly intoxicated, hiccuping attempts at the Greek names, I sought to . . . test their understanding of what had been read. The trouble was that my own understanding had been gravely undermined. To my unnerved questions they returned senseless answers. Something horribly like actual drunkenness now possessed my little charges.

I hurriedly switched to my lesson on London. More than anything was this to be a *lecture*. Miss Frome had startled me the day before by asking if I meant to give them maps and to encourage them to draw. 'You'll get them to collect pictures too, I imagine?' 'Yes,' I'd answered, amazed by the simple obviousness of such ideas, and by my simple failure to have hit upon them unaided. But now, working from my massive collection of notes, I meant to introduce them to the broad range of the topic. I saw, as I began to speak and caught confused glimpses of the impish faces in front of me – I saw at once that what I meant to say, this dense exordium, rested on a view of historical processes, on a simple assumption of interest in history itself, that was perhaps not natural to nine-year-olds. Some simplicity was required that was hopelessly beyond me. One or two broad notions . . . All I was prepared and able to offer was a thick mass of notions very narrow indeed.

We were in different worlds. In their world, they laughed incredulously, fought one another, played with their toy motorcars – read comics. I, in my world, juggled with my huge unsuitable load of facts and theories, and intermitted this with appeals, threats, statements of my amazement. The noise grew, positively as if it were water rising within the walls and we were all drowning. Scraps of my lesson floated this way and that on the surface of this outrageous sound. In despair I began drawing on the board: a map of Roman London. It was my first attempt to draw a map with chalk on such a surface, and the unforeseen sideways nature of such work startled me. Alone with the blackboard, undistracted, I should have had problems. In the midst of all that noise, my head buzzing with dreadful thoughts – so I wasn't even going to last a day, a morning! – they would surely at any moment come and take me and thrust me out through the main door! – in such circumstances, the parts of the map failed to unite: it wasn't London at all, it was a sort of cartographic goitre, misleading in the extreme. I tried to write a title above it, and the words took their own course from the top left-hand corner down towards the bottom right-hand corner. Said a voice: 'We've never had such a lesson before.' Another, hysterically satirical: 'We've never had such a nice lesson.' The cue taken up elsewhere: 'We've never had such a *nasty* lesson.'

At this point a boy ran up to me and thrust an arm through mine. He then turned to the class and said: 'This is my uncle.'

'Sit down,' I cried, attempting to untwine this dreadful child's arm from mine. But he clung on with astonishing strength. Then he swung his legs off the floor, so that his whole weight depended from my arm. I sagged sideways, and from this position continued my incredulous remonstrances. But he cried: '*Let's all swing on uncle!*'

The bell went . . .

I had entered that first week at The Vale expecting the worst. I thought it absurd of Mr Juniper to appoint a man wholly untrained and inexperienced, even to play the minor role planned for me. I thought it quite unaccountable on his part to appoint someone to whom the world of prep school and public school was totally unfamiliar. If I was carried along, it was by a sense of not being at my own disposal (a feeling with, in my case, deep roots), coupled with a curious satisfaction in finding myself cast for so improbable a role. 'Once more he demonstrated his tragic versatility in masquerade . . .' 'He refused no impersonation pressed upon him, however bizarre. Indeed, the more bizarre the better . . .' I'd always had the habit of justifying what was happening to me by making phrases for it out of fiction. If I could turn myself into a character in a novel, then it was possible to carry on.

It would be painful, I foresaw, that first week, and I would make many uncomfortable mistakes.

In the event, the stunning nature of my sense of failure and humiliation staggered me as much as if I'd expected to do well. I'd braced myself for a beating, and was pole-axed instead.

Said Miss Frome: 'Oh, don't look so depressed!' But I could not smile. I wanted nothing so much as to rush into Mr Juniper's presence and cry: 'It's no good! I can't do it!'

Prominent among my feelings, as I trudged over to the senior school to complete that dreadful morning, was one of horror at the idea of exposing children to such grotesque ineptitude and noisy, unprofitable farce. How could that be justified! I felt that in an hour or so I'd already ruined Middle Three's education. Oh really: I must, I thought, for all my self-deprecation, have imagined I should do well enough: or rather, that if I did badly, I should be no worse than a poor apprentice teacher. That I should turn out to be a non-teacher – worse, an *anti-teacher* – was an idea that hadn't entered even my mistrustful head.

I heard Rose-M explaining to the darkly handsome Squadron Leader lying beside her on the Cornish cliff: 'Oh, you've no conception! Fifteen little boys aged nine could destroy his authority in five minutes...'

When I'd renewed my inquiry about Upper Five History, Mr Diamond had thrust a textbook into my hand. 'First ten chapters of that will cover it, young man. The Middle Ages. Fill their heads with facts. That's the way we do it. You can't go wrong if you focus on the facts.'

I'd read the first chapter of the textbook with dismay. It was so exclusively full of facts that it had the indigestible quality of a dry meal. The gravy of a few general ideas and a little relaxation of style and speculation would make it more suitable for Upper Five, I reflected, let alone for their haplessly unqualified teacher. I had resolved to read that first chapter with them, but to attempt to add a little juice to the arid dish by way of commentary and even – hmm – scholarly pleasantry.

That was how I'd thought of it before the earlier events of that shattering morning. It had been vague, worried, unconfident. But it had been a plan, to cling to.

They addressed, as I entered the room, cheerful remarks at me that I could not mistake for the currency of a properly conducted classroom. Within a moment I knew that my problem had been re-asserted: the problem, so remote from any prospect of solution that it didn't even seem urgent, of discovering some way of asserting my will over that of any group of boys. Oddly, on that morning's complex scale of panic and despair, this period with Upper Five did not represent the depths. I'd thought it must do so. But there had been a curious awfulness at being unable to control fifteen nine-year-olds that was not topped by the numb discovery that I could not manage sixteen twelve-year-olds. They at least did not collapse into an infant's hysteria. They were chummily impossible.

And at once one of them cried: 'Sir, can we copy the plan of the old monastery on page 63?'

'Ooh yes,' cried others with fervour. 'Ooh sir, what a smashing suggestion of Cuffe's! Mr Diamond would be most gratified!'

'There's no need,' I essayed, 'to—'

'Tracing paper in the cupboard, sir!'

'Oh well, then. I had in mind—'

'I'll give it out, you stinking troglodyte!'

'Are you sure that tracing paper—?'

'You take it easy, sir, and leave it to us.'

The room was filled with unmonastic comments on the layout of a medieval monastery. Boys crowded round my desk, and their appeals for my help or for clarifications did not all ring true. 'Sir, would a medieval *convent* be much the same—?' 'Don't be a ninny, Pearson! Imagine a lav door in a convent with MONKS written on it!' 'Oh look, let's keep this serious and sensible!' 'Sir, Pearson's a notorious ninny about nuns!' 'Now, look here—*What's* that? What's that noise?' 'Oh, I *am* sorry, sir! My desk has this habit of falling over. The Leaning Desk of Upper Five, they call it.' 'Sir, it's obvious that they refected in the refectory, and one guesses what that is, but what did they cloist in the cloisters?' 'Oh, Digby, you're *so* humorous! Sir, pay no attention to Digby's *withered* wit!' 'Oh, I say, come on—!'

It was not, even by the most perverse reckoning, a lesson. It was a very noisy, foolish waste of time presided over by an incompetent with savage aches in heart and head. But in the fantastically wide torrent of this longest day of my life I had now reached the small midway island of lunch.

Mr Hollow roamed the staffroom, deploring the weather that made football impossible. There had to be an emergency timetable. His wrath was great. He looked constantly out at the wet world beyond the staffroom windows, hating the Labour government. I had already discovered that, among the staff of The Vale, Mr Attlee and his ministers were deemed to have Nature herself in their inept, seditious hands.

'D'm'd n'sance! W'st S'tember I c'n 'member! Oh, M'st' B'sley – k'p Upp' Four h'ppy, eh?'

As I sat in the comfortable staffroom, on the edge of the least assertive chair I could find, I felt despondency on my face like a bruise. It was with the thinnest smile that I acknowledged Mr Hollow's suggestion that I confer impromptu happiness on Middle Four. I could do anything I liked, he seemed to be saying. Read them a story, if I wanted to.

That was what, of all the hideous alternatives, I most wanted to do. I took a book with an adventurous title from the crowded staffroom shelves. I went into Middle Four. I began to read.

I think I had not known till that moment how badly written a story may be, and yet get itself into print. The words here fell together in such a way as baffled the tongue and then the ear. The author was a master at putting words side by side so that each drained the entire quality out of its neighbours. The narration was amazingly inept – at every twist and turn the story was leapt upon by the writer's incompetence and smothered in a blanket. My voice ached with the effort to give it meaning and flight. Middle Four appeared dulled – at no point entirely ready to admit that a story could make them so wretched: until near the end, reasonable in their twitching half-attention.

'This author,' someone muttered inside my shrieking skull, 'has not been able to distinguish between giving a story suspense and hanging it by its neck until it is dead.'

My sense of being quite grievously damaged had now spread from head and heart to vocal cords. Nothing worse, I thought as I crept away from angry Middle Four, nothing worse could follow. Whatever came now, in this phenomenally protracted day's last period, must have some quality of anti-climax, or at worst of repetition.

But what actually happened next was that I was sent to supervise Lower Six prep. It was an experience I could not bring myself to think about till days later.

4

Term had begun on a Wednesday. I spent the weekend divided urgently into three incompatible persons. One was stunned, unwilling to reflect on what had happened. Another was desperately attempting to arm himself for the week to come; this one was positively writing out, word for word, his lessons for Monday, Tuesday . . . The third was trying to see, and trying to avoid seeing, Rose-M.

We had, in a fashion, communicated during her absence in the West. I had, indeed, written thousands of words to her, mostly unposted. These aborted letters of mine followed a pattern. First I wrote pure singing declarations of love. These were addressed to a Rose-M enormously simple and warm. I teased her, trembling. 'How could so long a nose and so cold a nose be so lovely a nose?' Having written such a thing, I'd be pulled up sharp – with a different sort of trembling. True, in a certain confusion at one of our meetings that I could not be sure was accident or, on her part, erotic engineering – on that occasion, there'd been . . . protracted facial contact. 'Yer Honour, there was protracted facial contact between the accused' . . . Oh, I was a fool, surely. In her circle such accidents relating to the face were probably common and meaningless. Only an infatuated fellow from a lower social level would not only read significance into such a thing, but base upon it lyrical sections of unsolicited correspondence. Because, indeed, she hadn't asked me to write to her, surely? She'd given me her address. But that might well be quite another matter.

'My dear, I gave the fellow my address and before I knew where I was, he'd written me a letter!'

So my simple lovings were followed, in the pattern of these unposted letters, by complex passages designed to throw the meaning of their predecessors into sophisticated doubt. I ran towards her, and then backed snickering away. A gush of new warmth would follow, would irresistibly form a letter's conclusion – sometimes forcing itself into postscripts and once into a sentence on an envelope already sealed.

I had still been writing and re-writing, a platonic activity in which the General Post Office played no part, when a letter came from Rose-M. 'It's lovely here – you'd love it especially. Lots of friends – but I could do with *one* or two more. Perhaps not so many as two. One of my ex-fiancés was here over the weekend – did I ever tell you about him? *Most* disapproving of what I'm now doing. Ah well! Do write and tell me what you are up to. One or two people have been *quite* interested when I told them I have a friend who's going to teach at The Vale . . .'

Pssh, I thought, on receiving this. Pssh! Oh dear! How brittle and— *One* of her ex-fiancés? My soul filled with the spirit of coarse rejection. Good heavens, what a . . . superficial child! I set my jaw and felt a thousand years old. Within ten minutes the phrases for a reply were running through my head. 'I would give anything to be there. Oh, Rose-M, to be on the edge of that great sea, to hear the sound of it, in your company. We'd climb, wouldn't we, up until the sea was a quaking floor below and the wind blew us together and—'

Cue, at once, for revulsion – for panic-stricken escape into sophisticated ironies – brittleness . . .

I wrote, in fact, a tightly belted, bristling letter, tuned to a foxy snigger. 'I shall be the world's worst teacher, do not doubt it . . .'

There had been a postcard during this first week of mine at The Vale. 'I am coming home on Friday. Would it be nice if you rang me and then came to listen to music over the weekend?'

It arrived when my experiences at The Vale seemed to have set me apart from the whole world. They seemed also to have made it improbable that I should have either the time or the nerve to listen to music again – let alone to engage in affairs of the heart. Those three days at The Vale had made it seem improbable that I had a heart, in the usual sense. I had a pump, no doubt, but it kept alive an incompetent – a ludicrous person capable of being bowled over by any loose grouping of tiny boys.

Tiny, yes! I was latterly astonished by their minuteness. These persecutors of mine, I would become now and then amazedly aware, were nine, ten, eleven years of age. The oldest were coming up to thirteen. Some were witty and sharp as I'd never expected small boys to be. Some of the sheer cleverness of that cerebral suburb had . . .

oh, not rubbed off on them . . . nothing so casual. They had become part of the general atmosphere of shrewd brightness and intellectual unexpectedness.

Mr Hollow had come into the staffroom chuckling furiously over a piece of prep. 'Draw the graph and give it a title,' had been the general instruction in one of the problems. A boy had written: 'His Most Royal and Eminent Highness the Lord Graph . . .' I felt at once unworthy to be the instructor of minds so amusing.

I had discovered a sanction: you could give a boy detention. You sent him, in fact, for the detention book, which lived in the head-master's room. I'd tried once, on that awful occasion I was still unready to think of when I supervised Lower Six's prep, to send a boy for it. As he stood sulkily at the door, crying: 'Why me? I've done nothing. I'm making a list of masters who give detentions this term and—' . . . as he stood there I was panicked, not by his threats but by the dread of confession to Mr Juniper, through this application for the book, that I was in trouble. Would he not come himself and say: 'Well, if this is how you're struggling and floundering about after only one or two days of term . . .' 'Come back,' I'd fatally ordered the boy frowning at the door. 'Come back and let's try to get on without that sort of thing.' His display of triumph had been appalling.

So I deprived myself of the only weapon known to me; though had I used it once during those early days I might well have used it a hundred times. I had no idea how little or much resorted to it was by my colleagues. But indeed the entire way of life of The Vale bristled, for me, with mysteries, inscrutabilities of procedure.

'Every other Monday, of course,' Mr Diamond had told me, 'there is Running-over.'

I had left it at that, for the moment. I didn't think this was likely to be a deliberately staged accident, or a ceremony involving the overfilling of some receptacle. But you never knew, at The Vale. Strange rites abounded. There had already been an occasion when Mr Capper had, after lunch, transformed himself, to my very great surprise (and, I rather thought, to his), into a scoutmaster, and had then dashed into the playground where he was waited for by a ragged and ribald square of cubs. Through the staffroom window I saw that he was shouting some ritual greeting, to which the reply came in a number of seemingly rather haphazard variants: he appeared dis-pleased by this. I turned away to continue with my nervous preparation of a lesson, and Mrs Leach was left as the only member of the staff looking out of the window. After a time, and with her customary precision, she said: 'Mr Capper has fainted, I think. At least, he has sunk to the ground and is lying there in a way that doesn't, *to me*, suggest consciousness.' I looked round at my colleagues, feeling there ought to be some response, and shy of being the first to rise and dash to the rescue. But the room was quite unaffected by Mrs Leach's announcement. Only later did I understand that people had simply got out of the habit of listening to her. A moment or two passed: then she said, 'I really *cannot* think that Mr Capper has adopted that position for any purpose connected with cubbing. Mr Hollow, may I recruit a second opinion?' Irritably aware of being addressed, Mr Hollow had crossed to the window with a cry of 'Ugh?' And so it was that Mr Capper, who had indeed fainted from too much indignation on top of too much lunch, was belatedly raised and carried in from the playground.

So there was no knowing what Running-over would amount to. My feeling, that I might as well wait and see, was converted to considerable alarm when Mr Hollow cried, as we passed in a corridor: 'H'pe y're g'v'g 'em 'ps 'n d'ns!' 'Eh?' I mumbled. ''Ps 'n d'ns,' bawled Mr Hollow, yards away. 'R'nn'g-over! Pl'nty 'ps 'n d'ns!'

I should be giving the boys, obviously, ups and downs. But what the devil were they? I worried at the question, off and on: but it was a grain in the choking dust of my general alarm. As in other fields, I shrank from making plain inquiries, so acknowledging ignorance. At bottom, I felt that such a phrase as 'ups and downs', used in this clearly special sense, must be ridiculously familiar to anyone whose true world was the world of The Vale. I maintained an anxious silence.

There was another nagging reference to it during that calamitous prep with Lower Six.

Unluckily, out of my misery and sense of displacement, I'd felt for a flash, in the staffroom directly before that experience, that in fact I perhaps did belong to the world of The Vale. Old Mr Raisin had quoted some Milton at me, from inside a curious existence as of some living anthology that, in the depths of a fat armchair, he led in the staffroom. It had thrown me when Mr Raisin had first addressed me in this fashion. 'Ah, miserable and unkind, untrue, unknightly, traitor-hearted! Woe is me!' he'd mumbled in my direction: adding, to what I took to be a picturesque outburst of uncontrollable hatred, a most charming smile. 'Ah,' I'd said, trying to smile back: and had hurried away and thought things over and decided, with some difficulty, that Mr Raisin had been quoting Tennyson. On this second occasion I was ready: and as luck would have it, I managed to continue the quotation for a line or two. 'A man of culture rare,' Mr Raisin had said, beaming: and it was then that Mr Hollow had stepped over and grunted:

'Take Low' Six pr'p. Hmmm?'

I went down steps into a little room off the hall, feeling that I positively shone: a man of culture, indeed, Eng Lit held in the palm of his hand. It was, in the shattered general state I was in, a moment of pathological light-headedness, perhaps. Somehow I believed, and this increased the shock to come, that the sixth forms, close to that all-deciding Common Entrance exam or those awe-inspiring scholarships, would be unlike classes elsewhere in the school. They would press ahead, self-driven, and the master in charge of prep would be the idlest of invigilators. I walked, then, to the master's desk, and became aware that the room was silent. It was another kind of silence than a preoccupied one. I was not accustomed to silent classrooms. I also realized that the jaw of every boy in the room was hanging down as in idiot inquisitiveness. The uniformity of this was disturbing. Indeed, I quickly decided that it could not be accidental. No, even I could not be persuaded that fourteen boys would hang their jaws in quite that way at quite the same moment without some collusion. But I was still the young man of natural brilliance, come from a humbler world to dazzle the aristocrats.

'Oh, don't be donkeys,' I cried, almost gaily.

They brayed then, very loud and very long. A boy with a dark face leapt up and laid his stretched hands beside his ears, making longer ears. Another turned and bent and raised an imaginary tail. The braying turned to a long farting. The boy with the dark face used his palm to prop an imaginary extension of himself, and let his eye run up and up along its invisible length. Aghast, I leaped to my feet and cried: 'Shut up! Shut up, at once! Shut up and get on with your prep!'

A voice said: 'Shut up is a very rude phrase!'

The dark-faced boy said: '*Bloody* rude!'

'That's enough!'

Three or four voices together, then: 'Blind man's buff!'

'That will do!'

'Timbuctoo!'

I skidded to a halt at the edge of this abyss of rhyme. My own jaw hung.

The dark-faced boy said: 'We'll all get downs.'

'Don't be daft,' said his neighbour. 'He can't. Doesn't take us.'

I said, with panic-stricken violence: 'If you don't get on with your work . . .'

'*The Angry Turk!*' The whole room had joined in, this time, and the laughter that followed, with other assorted expressions of glee, was enormous. Only some weeks later did I discover that *The Angry Turk* was the name of the pub whose attractions were held (quite falsely) to lie behind certain of Mr Hollow's arrangements of the timetable.

It was no man of culture, rare or otherwise, who left that terrible room. This seemed the final pointer to the improbability of my being, as a teacher, anything but a grotesque failure. My presence in a classroom was such that even young geniuses on the brink of the gravest experience of their lives were moved to folly – and even, I recalled with a shudder, to obscenity.

But some time or other I must discover the meaning of ups and downs.

If I was at sea when it came to handling a group of boys, I was plainly drowning when it came to the management of my contacts with a single girl.

I explored in my dazed head, that Saturday, the idea of ringing Rose-M and . . . And what? There was the rub! Would she not say: 'Come to tea. Mummy and daddy will be there, and a number of daddy's business friends, and – oh, a handful of handsome young military persons of my acquaintance, including an ex-fiancé or two . . . oh, and several dancers from the academy. All the men, by the way, will be wearing finely tailored lounge suits. I thought you'd be glad of the hint, dear Edward. I have told them that you will hold forth at length about the experience of teaching at The Vale. They are *agog*, my dear!'

No, no, of course not. Of course she would not say such things as these. Instead she would—

Instead she would say: '*Edward?* I beg your pardon . . . have you the right number? I can't quite recall anyone . . .'

Her father would answer. 'Look here, young man; what sort of bounder are you, to ring my daughter on the flimsy ground that she wrote and asked you to do so? Does it not strike you that if every young man to whom she was kind enough to write such a letter actually did ring her . . . ?'

I let Saturday go, deeply dismal. James visited me during the evening. My parents were out and he performed, on our piano, an outline of an improved version of the slow movement of Brahms's Fourth Symphony on which he happened to be working. It was improved in the general direction of its being transformed into a fast movement in a decidedly uncertain key. When this was over, I attempted to convey to him the horror and guilt of my first three days at The Vale. 'My dear fellow,' he said when I'd finished, 'your imagination will bring you either to an early grave or to a long stay in a mental home. You honestly have a dreadful habit of working yourself into a stew about nothing very much. A few sharp punishments would soon settle all that.'

I'd meant to go on and tell him of my intricate feelings of advance and retreat in respect of Rose-M, but decided against it.

On Sunday I persuaded myself that I must attend unremittingly to writing out my lessons for the following week. During the evening

I was filled with a sudden reckless longing that drove me to the nearest phonebox. I stared at the flushed coward in the mirror as I waited for a response from the other end. Rose-M's mother said:

'Oh, *Edward*! My dear, she'll be *delighted* to have a word with you, but I think she's washing her hair. Hold on – I'll find out.'

I heard the sounds of that foreign household, tiny, terrifyingly unfamiliar. 'Where are you?' – close at hand. Then distantly: 'Rose-M! – where *are* you?' A male mumble. A splinter of music. I imagined those curls smothered in a bubbling cloud of fragrant shampoo. Rose-M would say: 'Oh, curse the fellow!'

Instead, her voice, soft in my ear, as if she'd slipped into the very phonebox: 'Edward!'

'Oh,' I said helplessly. Then: 'Ah!'

'Oh, Edward, why didn't you ring earlier? I'd been looking forward to seeing you. Do you know, I'd not gone out this afternoon – though I was invited to go out – because I still hoped you'd ring and we'd see each other.'

'Oh my goodness' was all that emerged from the sudden black cloud filling my head.

'Why didn't you ring?'

I embarked on a tangle of would-be explanation. Then I saw that it was not matter for the telephone: it was a novel, a long passage of confessional autobiography.

Rose-M sighed briskly. 'You *are* an unusual person, Edward. I mean . . . Oh, but that's what's interesting.'

'I beg your pardon,' I said – not because I'd failed to hear her, but because I had no idea what the reply should be.

She talked brightly, breathily, then, of her holiday – 'You must,' she seemed to be saying at one point, 'come down to Cornwall some time and stay at the farm.' There were many things, I believed as I walked away at last from the phonebox, many things of this kind that she had said or seemed to say. They were things, that is, that pointed surely to her feeling that something more than casual friendship might exist, or come to exist, between us . . .

Dammit, I suddenly thought, she mustn't. As a young dancer, with a career to be made – requiring to dedicate herself to the stern and beautiful exactions of that art – she must not think of *marriage*. How beastly of me in my head to carry her, as I now knew I'd been doing throughout that conversation, to the very altar. Wasn't it bad enough that I was now the worst teacher in the world? Must I also be scheming to destroy the future of an artist young enough – she was two or three years younger than myself – young enough to depend on the self-control and wisdom of her older acquaintance to save her from the consequences of rashness and . . . disgraceful sexual impatience?

I must save her from herself, which might well mean saving her from me.

I shook myself a little, being so unexpectedly at this point in my thinking. This was a landscape I didn't recognize at all. Where had I come to, and by what route?

We were meeting at an Under Thirties occasion, the following Thursday. She had suggested an earlier encounter, at her house – 'On Tuesday mummy and daddy and my sister will all be out' – but I had a picture of the early part of the week to come: every evening would be taken up with a desperate attempt to foresee the chief dangers of the day to follow. 'No – let it be Thursday,' I'd said, wondering why she'd made such a point of those absences on Tuesday.

'Oh Edward,' Rose-M had said at the last, 'you are so unlike the men I've . . . Oh, never mind!'

Yes, of course— spiritually and emotionally cross-eyed and gammy-legged, I thought as I walked, slow with heavy speculation, away from the phonebox. A full moon was rising above a black wall of cloud and was throwing into the upper sky, as it did so, a hoop of scratched bronze. Oh, she was lovely, lovely, I thought, and her curls were the colour of scrapings from that shining echo of the round moon up there.

5

I discovered now – in that moment of pitiless self-understanding that comes when one wakes from a night's sleep – that I was afraid of the boys: afraid of these little scraps of children and their power to torment me and to thwart my edgy attempts to teach them.

I found myself shyly speaking of it to Harrod Parker, who was also new that term. I was in awe of him for his name: I'd not before met anyone who seemed sternly to have elected to be known by a pair of surnames. I thought that arrogantly aristocratic. But Parker was a thin, quick-minded, kindly man, who had behind him a long history of private tutoring. He'd not taught in a school, he told me, for twenty years or more. We compared notes, and he was good enough to pretend that his problems had been on much the same scale as mine.

'I think,' I said, 'you can't imagine—'

'Oh, it's frightfully difficult for anyone, at the start,' he said. 'I've worked out a little system, which seems to have *some* effect. I make anyone who misbehaves stand up – when six are standing up I threaten the whole form with detention, but give them the chance of working it off in the next lesson. Well, it seems to be a bit of a quencher.'

But that, I thought, was a complicated game that would sap all my stamina. I couldn't give my mind to such elaborate disciplinary ploys as well as to the problems of attempting to teach.

I gave an English lesson to Upper Three, the top form in the juniors. I'd worked out a reading of Harold Monro's poem 'Milk for the Cat,' followed by an analysis – simple, unforced, I thought it – of the means by which the effects of the poem were secured. The purring, milk-lusting, cat-descriptive verbs and adjectives . . . pointing to these, on top of the pleasure given by the reading, would form an illumination well within Upper Three's understanding. And again as I brought my careful plan face to face with its actual beneficiaries, my heart sank. Once more I'd misjudged my audience. In terms simply of vocabulary, the poem was beyond them. The whole notion that such verbal effects might be contrived, and that one might be interested in the way it was done – this too was outside their natural appetites. Even as, faltering and aghast, I made my way through the lesson, thrusting it forward unhappily against the dull wall of their bewilderment, I began to have a little more understanding of the simple, bold strokes in which the teaching of such little boys ought to be conducted. Depression seized me. I could not make myself indifferent to the irreverent comments in which they sought relief. 'In these words, can't we *feel* and *hear* the sound made by the old ladies' silk dresses?' 'Can you hear anything?' a boy asked, leaping up and addressing the entire class. Another put his ear to the ground, Indian-fashion. 'I can't hear a thing!' The room filled with purrings, rapidly mated with bow-wowings.

I tore up sheets of paper and angrily gave them out: then launched into an ill-considered test on parts of speech. With shame I realized that my mood was that of a man who says: If you can't enjoy the beautiful, gay programme I'd worked out for you, with great expense of thought and time, then you shall have a thoroughly nasty and dull and slightly brutal programme in its place.

It was still wet: the football grounds were waterlogged, and Mr Hollow continued to pace the staffroom after lunch, cursing the decline and fall of the British climate. Mr Raisin and I took a long crocodile to the peak of one of the suburb's green hills. There German prisoners-of-war were levelling the site of a demolished air-raid shelter. I'd worked with such men on the land, and amid my babbling boys I felt an overwhelming nostalgia for the companionship of these exiles, for the odd exercise of attempting to speak their language, for the irresponsible character of their labour . . .

I felt easier for a morning: not tightened into a nervous knot. I seemed calmer, positively capable at moments of quelling outbreaks of noise. I was not even thrown when Blossom ii, in my Middle Three, rolled up to my desk before assembly – a round, lazy boy – and accused me of being chickenhearted. 'You know, sir? – you're chicken-hearted. You want to *tell us off*! The mistresses do. And you're a *master*!' 'Ah, Blossom,' I said. 'Do you really expect me to be more formidable than the ladies?' He made nothing of this, but patted my hand paternally. 'You want to try not to be chickenhearted,' he said.

But the unforgiving ghosts of my earliest performances were constantly appearing to undermine these tiny interludes of confidence. Chief among these was the dark-faced boy of my experience with Lower Six, supervising prep. On duty in the senior playground, I was followed everywhere by this boy, who filled my close neighbour-hood with hostile gestures thinly disguised as attempts to blow away imaginary clouds rising from my pipe. Then he was at my heels, very close indeed, and I turned and cried: 'You will do me fifty lines for impertinence.' 'You can't, you can't,' he cried. 'You don't know my name, so you can't.' He vanished then, but contrived to be for the rest of that playtime a face half-seen between others, a farting noise from behind me.

Then came my first boarders' supper.

Masters stayed, according to a weekly rota, to supervise this occasion. Miss Pumphrey, the matron, smiled happily when I arrived in the corridor leading to the hall. 'They'll try to chip you,' she said. 'They always do a new master.'

I was fascinated by that word 'chip'. It was not descriptive of the torments with which The Vale had made me familiar. I smiled back, in a gloomy fashion, and went into the hall. The tables, with thirty boarders scattered among them, were screeching. From the walls, painted parsons and soldiers evaded my eye.

All the worst boys, I saw at once, were boarders. There was, for example, a whole tableful of my tormentors from Middle Four. At their head was a boy called Hazard, who had cultivated, for my benefit and as a greeting, a species of hysterical shriek. A small boy, black of hair and eye – an altogether dark, frenetically menacing child, enormously spoilt – he practised a general art of screams and screeches. And the mischief of his friends took its cue, one way or another, from his. So Dennis went in for whispers. Hazard would be calling out near-impertinences at the shrill top of his voice, and Dennis would fill in with insolent mutterings. I'd say: 'What's that, Dennis? Come on – what did you say?' and he'd shrink away, nervous and defiant and sly. Hazard meanwhile would have clapped a hand across his own mouth and cried, 'Sorry, sir! Oh, sorry! *Sorry*!' 'What's all that about, Hazard?' But meanwhile Dennis would have resumed his whispers. He had one of the school's least likeable faces, marked by this expression of cowardly cunning. 'What's that, Dennis? Come on – what *did* you say?' Working together, they could keep on the boil the tempers of teachers much more experienced than myself.

I murmured grace, and supper began. The noise remained steadily appalling. I stayed by the serving table, inhaling the excellent smells of the food and hoping that nothing much would happen. But from Hazard's table I thought I could hear abusive fragments and distortions of my name. I moved carefully towards it and tried to fix Hazard with my eye.

It was a mistake. He retaliated at once by fixing me with his, which became immense: a huge orb filled with malice. I frowned. Dennis was murmuring busily. Without looking away, Hazard nudged his other neighbour, Lightfoot ii.

Lightfoot ii provided a further voice in their fugal approach to mischief. He was laconic and cracked of tone. His hoarseness he managed like a musical instrument: he could make his voice grate and creak, horribly. He had one solemn interest in life: cricket.

Now, feeling Hazard's elbow in his ribs, he croaked: 'You bugger!'

Hazard seized the flesh at the corners of his eyes and stretched it, at the same time driving his eyeballs deep into the long apertures thus achieved. 'Mr Blishen,' he shrieked, 'was looking at me like this. Mr Blishen's eyes went haywire. I think Mr Blishen is going mad.' Dennis muttered and giggled. 'You've made me drop half my supper on my lap, you bloody loon,' said Lightfoot.

I walked across to the table. 'That will do,' I ventured, referring to the entire incident. Then I attempted to separate crime from crime and to forbid each one. 'There will be no making faces, Hazard. There will be no rudeness. If you want to speak, you will speak *clearly*, Dennis. You will watch your language, Lightfoot.' Lightfoot seemed to be genuinely puzzled. 'Watch my language? What's he talking about?' Then he added: 'Hazard, you loony bugger, you've made me mess up my best flannels.' 'I think Mr Blishen's seriously ill,' said Hazard. 'What shall we do if Mr Blishen *collapses* and *dies*?' 'Is Mr Blishen dying?' asked Lightfoot, with sudden interest.

'Oh, get on with your supper,' I cried, defeated, helpless. Matron, waiting at the serving table for the arrival of the sweet, looked across at us with what seemed a distinctly uneasy smile. I moved away, affecting a careless air and stumbling over . . . a foot, surely? Yet there was no foot visible as I managed to break my fall by clutching at the nearest piece of furniture. This turned out to be a table on which, among other things, the bell stood. The table tilted and the bell fell to the floor, hideously jangling. A boy ran and retrieved it and in doing so managed to ring a vigorous peal. From Hazard's table came a massive shriek – fugally sustained and embellished.

I became aware of Mr Juniper's figure in the gallery above. He was peering down at us. How unruly, I wondered, did the scene appear? How could I guess what orderliness and whispering meekness might be achieved by other masters on supper duty? I tried to smile up at him. 'Masters shouldn't make faces at the Headmaster,' called a voice. 'Ahem,' said Mr Juniper. It sounded worse than a full-scale impeachment. He disappeared.

'And now, complete silence,' I cried, furiously . . .

When they'd gone, I stood amid the hastily piled crockery – I should have seen that it was neatly collected, but that was beyond me – and wondered again how I could possibly go on. I was being paid £200 a year for the privilege of being extensively humiliated by little boys from quite another social shelf than my own. What *was* the sense of that?

They'd gone up the stairs, shrilling, towards the staffroom, eager for the evening's instalment of the radio serial *Dick Barton*. It had been like the last rotating uproar of water disappearing into a plughole. Need I join them? My briefing was to stay until the younger boys were fetched by matron. I enjoyed the silence of the hall for a little longer, as if it were some narcotic. Then I went upstairs.

As I opened the staffroom door I half-expected a booby-trap to crash down on my head. But they were all round the wireless set: I had been completely forgotten.

I leaned against a bookcase, weakly, and made a mental note of a necessary revision of the dictionary. '*Chip*, v.t. To torture, to subject to ingenious malice, to destroy a person's morale.'

A long sequence of overnight rains came to a halt, and I experienced my first game of football.

It was with juniors, and I was paired as supervisor with Mrs Cakebread, a gentle, amused woman whose instinct was to make people feel as important as possible. So she said, when I joined her that afternoon: 'They *are* lucky, you know – having a master to take them. It will make all the difference, I'm certain.'

'Mrs Cakebread,' I said. 'I wish you wouldn't think along such lines. I'm not really going to be . . . I'm not likely to be much good, you know.'

Mrs Cakebread smiled at me gently. I had now just about enough confidence to believe that it was indeed a friendly smile, and not one springing from Mrs Cakebread's knowledge that, as a master in charge of football, I was an outrageous impostor. I even toyed with the idea of telling Mrs Cakebread that I didn't understand football: that my attempts to read it up, in more than one manual, had left me knowing rather less than when I began. I wanted to say: 'Oh look, dear Mrs Cakebread, among the varieties of imposture I've brought to my work at The Vale, this business of being in charge of a game of football is worse even than the fraudulent character of the part I play in teaching itself, or cubbing, or . . .' But I saw that, convinced though I was of Mrs Cakebread's sincerity and sympathy, this was too much to inflict upon her by way of confession.

On the field I relied on her altogether for some theoretical grasp of the game. I put myself physically in the middle of it, with my whistle, very willing to run up and down in the neighbourhood of the ball so long as Mrs Cakebread was somewhere within earshot, calling: 'Now, pass, Rees-Rose! Oh do pass! To your wing! To your *wing*!' I myself uttered cries and grunts that might be taken for assents to such urgings, or utterances overtaken by Mrs Cakebread's own. It seemed to work – there were no positive complaints from these determined scrimmages of small muddy boys.

But the game, I could see, might be the least of it. There was first, at the junior school, the gathering of the players. For all the expertise of the junior school ladies, this was like trying to organize a flock of birds for some un-birdlike purpose. Chittering, fluttering, they'd come together and then scatter again, and it was a tedious time before at last we were on our way to the sports ground. No public line of boys from The Vale, I was to discover, was ever easy to be with, but this was perhaps the most difficult. They developed unforeseeable passions for unexpected features of the journey. Suddenly they'd have become a shrill cluster outside a women's outfitters – discussing, with great candour, the garments in the window. They might well be suddenly on their knees, peering into a drain. Amazing impulses would take them down some hopelessly unsuitable road, from which they had to be herded back to the correct route. Some of the time they were jostling for possession of my hands. Mrs Cakebread, tender though she was, had developed the sensible junior school lady's immunity to this clutching for a teacher's hands. But mine were asking to be fought for. Mrs Cakebread sighed over this, rather, but seemed to take it as further evidence of the advantage conferred upon me by being masculine. She intervened only when once or twice I was in the clutch of more than two boys, one on each side. I was dismally certain that again I was permitting a fearful distortion of the correct teacherly image. I ought not to have been so held, however dignified the holding. But it was never that. One of my captors, not releasing me, would hurry backwards, to throw a remark into a conversation occurring to the rear. My other captor would hurry forward, wanting to catch up with Mrs Cakebread. I'd be torn in two: or would find myself trying to remain upright, and in a safe and sensible position vis-à-vis the traffic, while my captors were examining something in the gutter.

When we arrived at the ground it turned out that the laces of their boots, knotted together so the boots could be made to hang round their necks, had been so tethered since the last game a year before. 'Sir, my laces! Sir, quick – undo my laces!' I hurried up and down the twittering line, my fingernails shredded.

Mrs Cakebread sighed with pleasure as, at the end of that first afternoon, we neared the junior school again. 'You *did* make *so much* difference,' she said. I was too tired to remonstrate. I was feeling, indeed, a little odd pleasure myself. Unexpectedly, I'd enjoyed all that running up and down, in the bleak September air. It was good to have my limbs in use again . . .

And that was a week of it, then. A week of shrill din, of the most intense nervous strain I'd ever experienced. It was, I thought – sitting bruised in the trolleybus on my way home – a lost, frightened week, on the whole. Oh, I'd surely never find happiness in school teaching. I felt so irritable, *irritable* – unable, at home, to endure questions about The Vale. To these I gave snappy, sulky answers.

Close to sleep, I imagined the hostile reports heaped on Mr Juniper's desk. In what shape would my dismissal come?

6

The great dismay of my life at The Vale had strengthened my longing for Rose-M. After six weeks I had no clear memory of her face: yet with some image of her I had, all that dire week, conversed. I'd imagined her anew – sweet, tender, perfectly understanding – an invention supported by a few half-remembered realities. I yearned towards our meeting, as if it would blot out all distress and pain under some immense bliss.

It was a debate that evening, at The Under Thirties. A polite, uneasy debate, on a matter of small importance; and it rapidly petered out. I sat with James and was miserably glad that we were at some distance from Rose-M. When the debate had died, I talked loudly to my companion, somehow hoping that I appeared grandly indifferent to the rest of the company. James said: 'You *are* excitable this evening, old chap; I'd advise you to take a deep breath.' He made his way over to a group that included Rose-M, and leadenly I followed.

She was telling some story about her dancer's day. '*Incredibly* nice person,' she was saying. 'Really, everyone *adores* him! All those tales they tell about him are *so* untrue!'

Italicized fiddlesticks and gush, I thought wretchedly. The people round her looked blank, as if – as seemed most likely – they'd never heard of the man, whoever he was, whose adorable nature she was asserting. My entire fabrication of hopes fell flat at once. This wasn't anything like the voice I'd heard in my head since she set out for Cornwall. That had been soft, sensitive, most secret, most amused. This was a shallow public patter . . .

My sleeve was being plucked and it was James. He said: 'Miss Perkins has been standing patiently at your elbow for a full minute. Good evening, Miss P – I apologize for my friend.'

I turned to give her a glacial smile, and at once fell deeply into the world of her presence: a world of coppery curls, of bright eyes and – oh, what to say of her mouth?

'Edward,' she said. 'How was teaching?'

I wriggled, half-laughed, was possessed by instant gloom: shrugged my shoulders. 'How is dancing?' I stammered.

James took over and, having briefly referred to my feverishness – 'I find the poor fellow frankly impossible to talk to' – began to speak of some theories he had in respect of an ideal performance of Verdi's *Otello*. Rose-M leaned against a wall and smiled up at him. I found myself, somewhere in the trembling centre of my existence, pondering the problem of her nose. There was only one word for it: sharp. Yet if you wrote, 'She had a sharp nose,' a displeasing picture would be conjured up. Clearly you could have a *beautifully* sharp nose. Well, Rose-M had. Her whole face . . . oh look, her whole face was based on some principle of sharpness, wasn't it? The cheekbones, so triangular: the chin, so like the toe of an elegant shoe. Wasn't it all this that gave that curious charm to her smiles – the appearance of new piquant angles among the rest? And then, it was all set amid curves – the curlings of her hair, and then the roundness of her neck, so that there was this little nest of angles, her face, found among these other soft, curving shapes . . .

We were walking towards the parish church. Ten o'clock was striking. I had gone to school under the shadow of that church, close to those chimes. It was as if I wore the church tower on my wrist. But indeed there were fingers enclosing my wrist, and they were Rose-M's. James was distinguishing the common run of Desdemonas from his own view of that tragic woman.

'. . . usually portrayed as such a feeble ninny,' he was saying.

Not for the first time I was struck by the gulf between James's prosaic personal life and the great tragic situations in musical drama to which he gave so much of his . . . yes, somewhat bullying attention. I could imagine him saying to any actual Desdemona: 'Look, my dear, you must try not to get so worked up about every accident that befalls your haberdashery. I think it might help if you came dancing with me on Saturday . . .'

Once James had turned this inappropriately majestic attention of his to philosophy. He had gone to an evening class; and in no time

43

he was bending the great issues of existence to the will of his bossy logic. 'But James,' I'd been driven to protest. 'All this talk of Being, with its capital letter, would seem so much more useful – my dear chap, don't be too much annoyed – if one was convinced that you had much to do with being, without a capital letter. I mean, if in everyday affairs you seemed a little more steamed up about things.'

It wasn't easy to annoy James. 'That's literary sloppiness, you know,' he'd observed, mildly.

Now his voice boomed on as we turned into the passage that led, through the churchyard, into the High Street. 'This will particularly interest you, Miss P,' said James. 'I mean, you must often have wondered about Emilia . . .'

'Ah,' said Rose-M. Her fingers seemed to be speaking at my wrist. They seemed to be saying that it would be marvellous if only we were alone. They were urging me, I thought, to use my ingenuity – or perhaps brute force – to drive James away.

But of course she couldn't mean that! What a hopeless person I was – building some such romantic structure of notions at the slightest . . . touch of a hand on my wrist. How dreadful, this incapacity of mine to make the acquaintance of a girl without imagining that I might marry her – that she might be instantly and overwhelmingly eager to marry me.

'Up there!' cried Rose-M suddenly. 'Edward, there!' I looked where her own gaze pointed, and saw on a ledge at the top of a building the shapes of a pair of pigeons. They perched there, side by side, faintly stirring.

'Breast to breast,' said Rose-M, and gave me a quick glance.

James had walked on, still talking. Now he'd become aware that we'd fallen behind; had turned to wait for us, no resentment in his face. James was a bore, but he had a civilized slowness in taking offence. He liked us both: he truly wouldn't expose his ideas on *Otello* to anyone with whom he didn't feel comfortable. But I wished him far away. I wished we filled him with unmanageable distaste.

He fell for much of the rest of the walk – through the town and into the sudden greenness beyond, where Rose-M lived – into one of his absorbed silences. I knew that when this happened, he was barely conscious of companions. So Rose-M and I whispered, off and on, exchanges that I was certainly doomed to bear away with me and brood over as if they were fragments of important literature.

'It seems,' I said, 'rather meaningless after a time – this putting one leg in front of another.'

'Can you think of better things to do?' she answered; and looked up at me in . . . surely a rather intense and significant fashion . . .

Later she wriggled: took her hand away from my wrist and fidgeted at her waist. 'My pants,' she said. 'They have a habit of . . .'

44

'My goodness,' I said. 'Can it be a common trouble? Surely in these days of improved elastic—'

'A tiny button, in fact, and a button hole not quite tiny enough,' whispered Rose-M.

' "The Willow Song," ' said James, breaking a long silence, 'can so easily be sentimentalized . . .'

He greeted with hearty delight the appearance of Rose-M's front gate. 'Well, there you are,' he cried. 'Hope I haven't . . . tried your patience. But I fancy you're the kind of girl who's interested in – er — Anyway, safely home.'

'Yes, *safely* home,' sighed Rose-M. Analysing the tone in which that was said, and its stresses – doing that alone would keep me busy, in the odd moments of a distracted life, until we next met. But I would also have to find time to consider the small and – surely not? – rather passionate speech addressed, as she turned to go, by her fingers to my startled wrist.

The following week had a general basis of despair, but I was beginning to manage it, even to be able to describe it to myself: like someone entertaining nervous hopes of taking charge of his own destruction.

I saw, for example, what a puzzle I must be to these little boys. My lessons on London had now taken sensible shape: I'd realized we must look at How London Grew: later at The Parks: The Bridges: The Tower of London: and so on. But I handled these topics with such agitation, such superfluities of talk and obvious lack of ease in respect of blackboards, pens, exercise books and the very way I might stand in the classroom, that my small pupils, anxious enough in the firm setting of the junior school to conduct themselves reasonably, were driven to noise and mischief.

My heart sank very far indeed one morning when out of the pandemonium a voice cried: 'You don't do this with the mistresses – why do you do it with the new master?' This charge was addressed by Blossom ii, who'd advised me to be less chickenhearted, against Paul Rackowski, a tiny, lively boy with a love of theatre. His family, I'd been told, were acrobats, famous and affluent circus performers, and little Rackowski had a general sinuousness and swiftness that spoke of . . . trapezes, tightropes. Among our reading books was a collection of simple plays, and Rackowski was always the first to put his hand up when I asked for a volunteer to read this part or that. Indeed his hand went up for every part in turn, long after he'd himself been cast. 'Look, Rackowski,' I'd say, 'you can't do everything'; but he'd smile at me and flap his hand above his head, obviously moved by a sense of logic quite different from my own. He took with the utmost gravity the author's directions as to the way in which a speech should be uttered. If ever this direction was beyond him – and it was a reading book with a poor sense of its young audience, so this often happened – he'd always produce something, by way of grimace or intonation. So it might say: 'PRINCE (*enigmatically*)', and little Rackowski would frown, sigh, and speak from deep inside his boots. I rejoiced in him, and was tormented by him: for my weak grasp of affairs at times drove him to strident ironies and unlawful acrobatic acts. When he came under attack from sorrowful Blossom ii, he allowed a whole parade of emotions to pass across his expressive face, and then turned a somersault. He did this too close to his desk, and ended in tears. I thought, dismally: When my own little nine-year-old pupils begin arguing with one another on my behalf in my hearing, then have I not sunk as low as it's possible to sink?

I was dismayed to discover that the senior staffroom was becoming a cowardly haven to me – and more. Once safely inside it I felt blooming within me the histrionic excitements of this unexpected role I was playing. A few months before I'd been a lorry driver's mate with a War Agricultural Committee – perpetually dirty, scarred. My ears were still full of rough rural voices. But now, in the staffroom of The Vale, I moved among voices polite and fastidious. I enjoyed this, despising myself for doing so, and noting with concern that I was beginning to talk in much the same way, and to walk about the room frowning in a delicate, preoccupied fashion.

I was more than ever struck by the resemblance between conversation in The Vale staffroom and the dainty sandwiches that appeared at the staffroom teas. My colleagues *handed round* comments to each other, with pleased little courtesies. 'Another remark about Czechoslovakia, Raisin?' 'Oh, thank you, Tooth!' 'Ready for an observation on Florentine art?' 'Oh, rather!'

What they said was so often so neat, so dismissive. I remember Harrod Parker and Eric Capper once concurring in the view that the entire Czech nation was 'dull and boorish'. 'Imagine it, Capper,' said Parker,' a community completely composed of boys like . . . who's that calvinistic little boy in Middle Five?' 'The most leaden-bottomed nation in Europe,' said Capper, firmly. 'Are you talking about the Czechs?' called Mr Beesley from a distant chair. '*Absolutely* the most *solemnly* uninteresting people!' 'One of the most unattractive of all the carols, when one thinks about it,' said Harrod Parker,' is "Good King Wenceslas".' 'How *perfectly* true!' said Mr Beesley. '*Insufferable* self-satisfaction!' They all glowed with the pleasure of being at one in their scorn.

You never knew where this scorn would alight next – or the reverse of it, indeed: their equally capricious approval. But often, not far away, you glimpsed the political feelings that influenced many of these bright judgments. So Mr Beesley, a man of obvious rectitude, would express vast support for all spivs and layabouts. 'In a day such as ours, so full of *dullards*,' he opined, 'we *desperately* need our idlers and . . . *flashy* fellows. Eh?' 'Some contrast, simply,' said Capper, 'to Ernest Bevin and that most colourless of Prime Ministers, Mr Attlee.' 'May I congratulate you on the accuracy of that adjective?' called out Mr Raisin, strugglingly, from his asphyxiatingly deep armchair. ' "Dull – beyond all conception – dull." ' 'What we need,' said Capper, taking strength from Mr Raisin's praise, 'is a widespread revival of the orgy, the practical joke and the large-scale, lighthearted crime.' 'Oh *rather*!' smiled Mr Beesley, who in fact was given to nodding at policemen in gratitude for the concern for his security that he believed them to feel.

I'd noticed this when walking to school one morning with this kindest and mildest of men – distinctly timid, except in these opinions of his. However, the fiercest of such opinions he would accompany with warm smiles. 'Karl Marx,' he once said to me, as the person nearest to him, and speaking out of a long inner fury of speculation, 'was quite one of the world's most *irritating* mischief-makers.' Then, smiling immensely: 'Could one really begin to add up the damage done by his *curious* reasoning?' Broader smile yet: and then he was up and off, humming happily.

Outside the staffroom, in the buzzing corridors and classrooms, I was undergoing every sort of agony. But once the heavy staffroom door had shut behind me, I was among such men as this one – this careful Mr Beesley, who moved about as though he were constructed of fine old china. You saw him walking to school with his umbrella feeling the pavement ahead of him – reporting back, you felt, on its surface, on the presence of hazards. He made his way about the streets like someone modestly precious.

In speech he avoided any directness: an umbrella was at work there, too, feeling an invariably circuitous way round the perils of straightforwardness. Sometimes one didn't easily take his meaning.

'Do you,' he asked me one day early in the term, setting his head in kindly motion, 'cultivate the cinema?'

'Cultivate it? Oh, go to the pictures? Ah! Often, indeed – often!'

Mr Beesley's roundabout phrases always set me gabbling. In the context he provided, one's plainer words seemed positively aggressive and coarse.

'Because,' said Mr Beesley delicately, 'I have been entertaining a small idea – have been on the brink of communicating a proposition – that I trust might be an agreeable one.'

'Ah yes. How nice!'

'Would it suit you,' asked Mr Beesley, 'on one of two or three coming evenings I shall later propose for consideration, after consultation in fact with Mrs Beesley, to accompany her and myself to the Phoenix?'

The Phoenix was the local repertory cinema. I had already developed a habit of escaping from the memory of a day at The Vale by spending an evening at the Phoenix. The most harassing tragedies unreeling themselves on the screen seemed a variety of light relief after some of my days of teaching.

I assented warmly to Mr Beesley's proposition. That's how I thought of it – it was no common terse matter of saying yes. In fact, here too Mr Beesley was feeling the way ahead: many months were to pass before this cautious exploration of, as it were, a future intention to explore further, led to an actual visit to the Phoenix with unimpulsive Mr Beesley and his wife.

Outrages abounded. 'This is,' I cried in Middle Four, 'a *disgraceful* form!' They burst into mass laughter and continued until worn out. 'It's so easy to laugh!' I roared, and they agreed with that: laughing again, twice as long.

Taking the dreaded Lower Six for prep, I'd tried to parry their jibes and to take the wind out of their sails by a display of lightheartedness. 'Get on with your prep so I can get on with mine' – that remark led to scathing discussion of a difference between us they thought I'd overlooked: that *I* was paid for the time I spent in that room. 'Oh, don't be so *very* bright!' I conjured my dark-faced enemy: who replied, 'I hope I don't dazzle you!' I fixed him with a stern glare, whereupon he twitched his eyebrows mockingly: there was widespread tittering. I lost all understanding of the situation, and when a boy called: 'May I leave the room?' I replied: 'What for?' They told me, happily and at lurid length.

I worried helplessly about 'ups and downs', about the whole system of marking. No one had thought to tell me about this; and I shrank from asking. I was still certain that to inquire about such things would be to confess scandalous ignorance. I'd be summoned to Mr Juniper's study. 'Anyone who hasn't possessed, almost from birth, a perfect understanding of systems of marking as adopted in preparatory schools of good standing, is no fit member of my staff! Go!' he'd cry.

In fact, my strong secret sense of criminal incompetence made me behave with the utmost nervous oddity whenever I ran into Mr Juniper or the junior headmistress, Miss Seakins.

At the Jewish New Year the school was half empty, and classes were combined. Mr Diamond, bustling into the staffroom with a deranged air – 'Great Scott, the whole timetable has to be reshuffled' – asked me to take a mixture of fifth forms for History. 'You'll only need to sit there, young man. I've told 'em to revise. All right?' What followed might well have been given some such title as Grand Comprehensive Demonstration and Display of Many Varieties of Impudence and Wild Behaviour. The air was thick with bizarre questions, songs and uncommon noises. Battles were fought; chases took place. I fell back helplessly in front of a growing tide of disorder. Five minutes before the period was due to end they swarmed towards the door, and I found myself monstrously standing with my back to it, attempting to hold them at bay. They were shouting and whistling. Surely the whole school could hear what was happening. Then through a door on the opposite side of the hall, Mr Juniper stepped.

I panicked. I opened the classroom door, uttered a few grave words – 'Well, that will do for now – I'll go into it further next time' – something of that order – and then, closing the door firmly but with difficulty against the loud thrusting mass, I walked forward to meet Mr Juniper. He said:

'Ah – where are you going, then? To the junior school?'

'Ah no. In fact, no. Not at all. Indeed, to the staffroom.' I was in the grip of a massive, ludicrous dignity.

'But the bell – I don't think the bell has gone yet, has it?'

I turned towards the table on which the bell stood. It was outside Upper Six's door; they had the duty of ringing it. 'Ah,' I muttered, as if visual inspection from a distance of six yards had failed to convince me one way or the other. 'I rather thought it had.' I noticed that the class I'd left made a hideously unsuitable spectacle as seen through the glass panels of the door. They were jammed there, mouths wide open, observing our encounter.

'Ah,' I said again, seized by some elaborate artfulness that seemed to be that of another person altogether. 'I think Upper Six's room is empty. That may be why the bell hasn't gone, if it hasn't.'

Mr Juniper looked more than usually impatient. 'Oh well, ring it then, will you?'

I strode over to the bell and shook it with majestic violence. Then, to my horror, I found myself grinning at Mr Juniper in a fashion that could surely only suggest that I was soliciting his amusement at these illegalities, uproars, outrages.

But he'd turned and was hurrying out of the hall at quite another corner. As if, I thought, his indignant uneasiness was too great to be grappled with anywhere but in private . . .

'You will find them charming,' a teacher friend had forecast. 'They will be from moneyed families or cultured ones – and if they are moneyed they will have been able to purchase a . . . specious culture.'

He'd looked at me severely. 'It is a world that could lead you to a certain – hmm – charming limitation of horizon.'

It led me, in fact, during my second week, to an alarmed attempt to digest a horrifying instruction received from Mr Juniper. Middle Four, he said, had a core of boys, perhaps I'd noticed this, who had difficulty in settling to any work whatever, but whose performance was especially atrocious in mathematics. There were nine of these boys, and he proposed to split them off three times a week from the rest of their class and put them into my hands. It would have to be in the staffroom.

It was of the usual order of Mr Juniper's sudden impatient ideas. Even as he spoke, a blackboard and easel went jigging and giggling past us, with Hazard, Dennis and Lightfoot ii in riotous command of them. 'Oh I say, you silly little fellows,' cried Mr Juniper, from the sight of whom they'd been cut off by their bulky burdens. 'Just take that along *quietly* for Mr Blishen. Who is it? Hazard? Hazard, you are a very foolish boy indeed, and waste a great deal of our time, do you not?' Hazard, unrecognizably small and meek, gave eager assent to these propositions. It struck me that perhaps to Mr Juniper things hideously clear to me – such as the carefully judged sly grin in Dennis's direction with which this modest self-accusation was accompanied – had become invisible. I was constantly astonished by Mr Juniper's apparent failure to observe so much, and was beginning to realize that, after forty years of teaching, the common or garden misbehaviour of boys might form an unremarkable part of the general atmosphere. He waved them on, and as he turned back to me I wondered if I looked as ashen as I felt. 'Hollow will tell you where to start with them, ' he said.

'V' d'tful ab't this,' said Mr Hollow, encountered in the staffroom. He wasn't at all convinced that it was a sensible experiment. I hoped he would not expand this statement. If he did so, must he not confess that, to his mind, education at its best did not consist in handing over deficient children to a deficient teacher? But Mr Hollow said no more: instead, he busied himself with snarling at Hazard, Dennis and Lightfoot ii. They were stupid little ruffians, I understood him to be saying, and positively the only escaped lunatics who during his long teaching career had ever attempted to erect a blackboard without ensuring that the cords that kept it from collapsing were properly taut. They could pick it up and next time he wouldn't regard it as an accident. The remaining six boys came into the room, clearly excited by the arrangement, and Mr Hollow increased that excitement by swatting at them in a general sort of way with a book, making savage speeches as he did so. The difficulty of being sure what he said gave the scene an appalling quality – as if the staffroom had been turned into some primitive jail – for all one could be certain of was that Mr Hollow was employing deeply felt phrases of violent and bitter abuse. They were seated at last round the staffroom table. Mr Hollow muttered in my ear – could it possibly be a word of condolence? – and, causing a final excitement by standing at the door and glaring like someone at the crisis of a Greek tragedy, left the room.

Long multiplication and division, he'd said. That's where I should start. I had hurriedly consulted myself and decided that I could more or less remember these processes . . . *Mathematics!* I had never claimed to be capable of teaching that! But to do so was not, as it happened, my first task in the staffroom that day. And it was my task only off and on throughout the miserable months of my duty as a remedial maths teacher. My main engagement was with the wild conduct of my nine pupils.

Hazard and Dennis were the brains, if the word is suitable, in respect of the way the mischief was organized, focused and made efficient. Lightfoot ii added his curious support, which consisted as always in his apparently recognizing no distinction between thought and speech. I would, in an odd moment of relative silence, be saying, perhaps: 'So the essence of it is this – to multiply by 100 you—'; and Lightfoot would say, with great clarity: 'That bugger Hazard has had second helpings every day this week. I'm going to see it doesn't happen today.' I'd roar at him for this, and Lightfoot would look amazed, as though most disinclined to believe that his stream of consciousness had turned into a publicly audible torrent. But Light-foot was far from being the noisiest of these boys. Even Hazard was left behind, in this department, by Nye. I think I have never met anyone more wholeheartedly opposed than Nye to intellectual exer-tion. In my presence he simply groaned – an expression of the coarse misery and impatience inspired in him by my ridiculous attempts to make him arithmetically active. Entering the room, he would turn his eyes upwards as if making some weary appeal for patience. Weariness was his forte: if I demanded any effort from him he re-sponded with a vast pantomine of fatigue, intended generally to suggest that he'd been brought very close to death by all . . . all this schooling. His own favoured means of passing the time consisted in the utterance of sudden cries, hoarse rallies of laughter, or bids to override the official proceedings with the telling of jokes that he'd just half-recalled. Attempt to bring any of these activities to an end, and he'd slump into his equally noisy weariness. He would yawn sometimes – enormous yawns that might have come through a megaphone. Nye had been known to utter one of these even at morn-ing assembly. . . For him, and a handful of other boys, The Vale had a phrase. They should, it was said, be 'in an elementary school'. The passage of the 1944 Education Act had brought about no change in this language. Mr Juniper said to me once: '*Don't* send that boy Nye to me

51

for anything whatever. He is . . . elementary school material.' I fancied he might have forgotten, or never understood, that I had myself been, in no figurative fashion, elementary school material . . .

But master of weariness though Nye was, he appeared vigorous by the side of Michael Loftus. Loftus's very clothes, I'd been astonished to observe, spoke of his inertness. Instead of having shaped themselves to the lines of an active body, as clothes normally do, they hung around him like some bell or balloon. The body inside was clearly too slack to make any impression on them, to cause the mildest creasing or bagging. Wearing a look of sad disengagement, he'd lean backwards in a chair, his mouth fallen open. His chief quality, outside this massive absence of energy, lay in his being, if caught in some impropriety, perfectly unabashed. Early in our acquaintance he'd suddenly made himself the cause of a curious lowing sound – a noise, at my elbow, strangely Alpine. I'd spun round and observed that he'd made a tube of his exercise book and was slowly blowing on its edge. 'What are you doing, Loftus?' I'd cried, being still addicted to this unhelpful and usually unnecessary form of question. At his leisure, and not obliging his head to the effort of turning in my direction, he'd answered: 'I am blowing on my exercise book, because I want to see what sort of noise it makes.' Then, in melancholy slow motion, he repeated the offence.

My embarrassment during these lessons was as great as it could be. The staffroom had large windows on two sides – one set of these staring into the playground, the other into the street. I felt like ducking out of sight at the appearance of every passer-by. On one occasion Mr Juniper himself peered in and almost at once arrived in the room, breathlessly critical of the angle of the blackboard. The boys' immense inattentions were replaced, at his appearance, by poses intended to suggest industry and profound respect for their instructor. To me these poses were wildly unconvincing, but again Mr Juniper seemed to notice nothing. He gave them, in a swift speech, a sketch of that system of unique privileges that had led to this arrangement – the provision of a special master to deal with their difficulties. 'Do your best – do your very best!' he cried, and then was off to bring his impatience to bear on some other corner of the battlefield.

But my worst embarrassment was that a master would from time to time elect to spend a free period in the staffroom despite my presence in it. My usual poor performance would be made very much worse by nervous shame. There were occasions when the knowledge that Mr Beesley or Mr Hollow was sitting in an armchair behind me turned my head into a buzzing emptiness. I did not know what to do next. Attempting to pilot Nye up and down one of these pyramids of figures that resulted from our study of long multiplication, I'd lose myself – stumble when half way up, suddenly distracted by what sounded like a scornful sigh from the invisible armchair, and come crashing to the foot of that mathematical mound. Nye would shout: 'I still don't get it!' I'd want to shout back: 'Oh for goodness sake, boy! – with the room full of critical observers, I frankly don't get it myself!'

On one occasion towards half term, when Mr Beesley was occupying that armchair, they behaved with a quite special devilishness. Hazard had hit upon the idea of accompanying his shrill cries with helpless slippings from his chair, so that he ended up under the staff-room table. Dennis, in response, had perfected a mumbling of condolences and a stretching out of helpful hands that somehow kept Hazard squealing under the table instead of hauling him to his feet. Lightfoot ii had been thinking aloud, on a number of revoltingly intimate themes, ever since he entered the room. Michael Loftus was frankly asleep; snores were being provided for him by a neighbour. With Mr Beesley in the room, I tried to deal with all this without giving way to apoplexy – my natural response. Verbally and physically I nipped and glared and hissed; I made faces intended to be eloquent of amazing punishments to come, once we were alone. At the end of the period I dismissed them and without looking at Mr Beesley – surely even that mild man's face must be distorted with scorn! – I hurried to my next lesson in one of The Vale's attic class-rooms. As it happened, this was with Middle Four reunited – my nine absorbed among their brighter but, as I saw it, scarcely less brutal peers. They put their excited moods together and set out to turn that classroom, poised above those grave and brainy streets, into a little bedlam. I found myself fairly gratified by this. I welcomed their wildness – would, had it been necessary, have stimulated it. Indeed, I think I did this: by roaring, for example, 'Stop it, you impossible, foolish boys!' and reaping my reward – a howl of laughter. I knew – if that's the phrase – my stomach knew that if they went on long enough, then quite terrifying qualities of rage would be at my disposal. Suddenly all the gathering fury of all these weeks would burst out of my soul like lava, like volcanic gas, and they'd all perish in the Pompeii of my wrath.

And so they did, in a sense. Five minutes before the morning's end the eruption took place, and one minute before the bell I had sixteen white-faced boys sitting in the shadow of my trembling angers. And I had sent Hazard for the detention book, and had not called him back. Whatever was the achievement of that very unpleasant morning, at least I had lost my ridiculous virginity as a giver of detentions.

7

I was, I sometimes thought, a butterfly being broken on two wheels at once. There was The Vale, one rotating torment. A wheel spiked with boys. Little Luke, for example, in my own form, Middle Three. Luke was, one could only say, deeply indifferent to the whole process of schooling. 'Still,' Miss Seakins had told me, 'under mother's microscope.' This had added nothing to my understanding of Luke. The junior school ladies were quick with such judgments – cryptic, most of them. They were like laconic distillations of, say, dossiers from Interpol. 'Rackowski? Hmm! Devil – or angel? Whichever it is, he's certainly dirty-minded.' That was Miss Frome speaking, and accompanying the dire epigram with her cubmistress's open grin. I wondered what phrase they had for me . . .

Well, Luke was watched over by mother, then. A beautiful, languid lady – I'd seen her – laden with brilliants. 'Christopher, dear,' she'd call, smiling her way into the home-going chaos of clucking boys, 'Christopher, are you ready to come?' And Luke would offer her his cheerily indifferent nod. That was what was so curious about Luke's indifference – its cheery character. He didn't care, but it was in the best of spirits that he didn't care. Under my tutelage, but one needed some other word, his written work became rapidly disgraceful. There wasn't much of it, and it looked awful. I'd attack it, bitterly; and pause in my tirade to observe that, as always happened, Luke was smiling at me in the most good-natured fashion. I had never before encountered such amiable apathy.

Their voices, their faces, filled my sleep. I was falling over a cliff and Luke was smiling, most pleasantly. Blossom ii stroked my face and murmured, 'You're the most awful bloody fool, sir.' Hazard came screaming wickedly out of the depths of a dream too awful to remember. Mr Juniper said: 'You will be solely responsible for Upper Six Greek.' He came into the room, where all the boys were smoking and reading comics. He glanced at the board, covered with my writing, and cried: 'That's not Greek! That's Latin!' He pointed to a corner of the classroom. 'You don't seem to have understood,' he fairly shouted, 'that I do not permit members of my staff to bring their young women to school with them.' Rose-M, I observed with a whole set of shivers, variously inspired, appeared not to be wearing clothes.

Rose-M provided that other wheel on which I was being broken.

Still we met only at gatherings of The Under Thirties – a setting with which I'd grown thoroughly impatient. I thought there were signs that Rose-M was bored, too, by those meetings. Not, I imagined, for my reasons – because those debates, discussions, talks so tiptoed round the edges of important questions. She was, I already knew, thoroughly in favour of intellectual tiptoe. I'd heard her charge the Labour government with heavy-footedness, 'Such a noisy crowd!' Then, observing my frown: 'Oh, Edward, you disapprove—' 'I was,' I said, 'trying to remember the last time I heard Mr Attlee being rowdy. Let me see, it was – ' 'Oh, you're spoiling for an argument,' she said, making it sound as though the marks of this condition were breaking out all over me, as visible as chickenpox.

No – something other than their insipidity was making her tire of those meetings. I thought it might have been the lack of the particular atmosphere of . . . oh, a saloon bar. But then, why did she stay with The Under Thirties? At times I found myself examining the idea that she did so because it . . . oh hell, how say this decently? . . . because it enabled her to meet me. I'd believe this for a dizzy moment or so; we'd be walking through the valleys of Wales – I wasn't quite sure why it was always Wales – there we were, walking into the sunset, eternally happy and compatible . . . and then shame and fear would fasten upon me. She was not of my kind – of course she was not of my kind. And I was not of *her* kind. Marrying her, I would take her into a world in which she'd be lost . . .

But self-distrust undermined every conclusion I came to. How bumptious of me to assume that there was this difference between us – this gulf. It was just, perhaps, that she belonged to people who didn't have to make a parade of their intellectual and artistic interests. I was a raw upstart who simply didn't understand the subtle and reticent world of the saloon bar, of the dinner table covered with napery (and drapery? was there a difference?), of the private telephone . . .

Reticent world of the saloon bar?

I had begun to walk through my own town sheepishly, ready tortoise-like to tuck my head down into the collar of my overcoat – ready to do that if suddenly round the next corner Rose-M should be, with her subtle, fastidious friends, a whole train of handsome lovers.

Then would come an Under Thirties evening, and from shame and shyness I would avoid her. I would stick close to James, feeling intensely unlikeable. The neurotic's sense, I told myself, that people would justly dislike him did they know what was going on inside him. That tug of war between condescending suspicion and desire. Yes, those whole teams of contending emotions: of longing, jealousy, the deep wish to be loved, the dread of forming a foolish union . . . Then, having been aloof, I'd spend the tail of an evening desperately attempting to correct the impression so made, watching for a chance to exchange smiles.

My bones still aching from one cruel wheel, I'd find myself strapped to the other. Miss Seakins said: 'You'll be delighted to know that you're a smashing teacher.' I recoiled as from some quite intolerable irony. 'Upper Three's verdict, expressed to me this morning,' she said. 'It's those twinkling eyes of yours. I do think you're lucky to have them. Bright eyes can't be faked, and they're worth a lot to any teacher.'

It took me a long time to believe that perhaps she was not being malicious. Like the indulgent yet sceptical guardian of an unhappy child, I allowed myself to be very cautiously gratified. At the same time I examined this proposition about twinkling eyes. I looked hard into a mirror, trying to establish the quality Miss Seakins had referred to. I tried to enlarge my view of the teacher and his equipment to include, as an important item, optical brilliance. But it sounded most unprofessional.

I thought little Tudor, as reported to me by Miss Frome, more perceptive. He was a gentle, sensitive boy in Lower Four, son of a distinguished musician and himself a cellist of promise. Little Tudor flinched from the hearty insensibility of most things, but he did so in a very manly way. He bristled with heroic intentions and ambitions, and had a particular desire to be notable at football. He was in my senior game, and always longed to be a captain; but was always appalled by the thought that he might be made one, and so run the risk of conceit and presumption. When the time came for choosing positions, he'd hang about in a tortuously undecided fashion, sometimes dashing forward so as to be certain of notice, sometimes attempting to hide behind taller boys. It was endless agony to little Tudor, this desire in all departments of life to excel and at the same time to efface himself.

There were occasions when, offered a captaincy, he refused it. 'No, sir! No, sir! No! No!' There were other occasions when, turning crimson in the struggle with his conscience, he undertook the office. Then, as often as not, a war would arise between his modesty and his wish to be at the heart of the battle. During his first game as a captain, I awarded his team a free kick. Tudor passionately wanted to take it; but he had a rival, equally and noisily eager. 'The captain decides who is to take it,' I ruled. Blushing with happiness, Tudor took the ball; then, in the grip of uncontrollable altruism, suddenly handed it to his rival. 'Here – you take it!' Then he ran to hide in the crowd, ashamed of his generosity, regretting his lost chance, horrified by the public character of the entire incident.

Miss Frome said: 'Little Tudor said an odd thing to me today. He said he wished Mr Blishen wasn't so unhappy. You're not unhappy, are you, old chap? You always look awfully cheerful when you're helping me with the cubs.'

So that's what twinkling eyes were, I thought. They were the impression given to superficial observers by the profound misery of my gaze and general expressions. Little Tudor was not deceived, of course. But then, his own nature must have taught him to look for improbable interpretations of contradictory human surfaces!

Tudor himself was at odds, I discovered, with the school secretary, Miss Cross. She considered almost everything that happened at The Vale to be absurd. Every feature of our daily behaviour was, in her view, a breach of common sense. She was short and stout, with dry grey eyes behind thick glasses. Her shortsightedness, which made it necessary for her to peer closely at everything, including faces, was a favourite weapon when she wished to draw attention to some aspect or other of the universal absurdity. She'd identify the passing face of a boy, bending down to do so, and laugh, snortingly. '*Him!*' she'd cry. I dreaded going into her office. 'Who is it?' she'd demand, testily, and do extraordinary things with her eyes, sometimes closing them altogether, as though my face were inconsiderately bright. Then: 'You!' she'd cry, and snort. 'Yes, Miss Cross,' I might say. 'I've come for half a dozen exercise books.' 'Exercise books?' Miss Cross would be amazed at the ludicrous nature of this need of mine. 'For boys to fill up with their scribble! All that writing, and those sums, and so forth!' She was specially down on such activities as these: elementary ones, without which one might assume nothing could be done at all. Thus you'd find her standing on the balcony, watching the boys pour down into the hall, up into the attics. 'All this moving about, and going from classroom to classroom!' she'd observe. Or, ringing the first bell of the day: 'All these morning prayers!'

Miss Cross thought human beings allowed themselves to become far too fanciful in their personalities. So she would bring her scorn to the way this boy smiled – 'Spend half his life *smiling*!' – and this other one walked – 'Came behind him this morning – one leg going in front of the other, left right left right, so absurd!' She regarded all but the most basic knowledge as a quite ridiculous acquisition. 'That's Mr Raisin holding forth down there, by the sound of it – in *Latin*, I suppose! *Latin!* I can't think why their own language isn't good enough for them!'

And when it came to little Tudor, Miss Cross made it clear that her feeling for the absurdity of his gifts as a cellist was too strong even to permit one of her amused snorts. It left her quite haggard, the thought of this modest little boy *sawing away* at his *fiddle*. Tudor, for his part, was deeply distressed by Miss Cross's refusal to give his instrument its correct name. It was a cello of some value, and when he brought it to school he left it, till needed, in Miss Cross's care. 'That fiddle again!' she'd cry. 'Put it over there, where I shan't see it!' 'It's not a fiddle, please, Miss Cross,' Tudor would insist, shyly but stoutly. 'Please, it's a cello. And please, you do know that, because I keep telling you.' Then he'd flush with the shock of his own daring, and begin to quiver. 'They're all fiddles to me,' Miss Cross would declare. 'But please—' 'All *fiddlesticks*!' she'd add, perpetually proud of this invention. 'Well, it'll be waiting for you when you want it.' Little Tudor would go out trembling and mumbling at the enormity of it, and at Miss Cross's appalling perversity. 'The time he spends shivering and talking to himself,' Miss Cross would say. 'And fiddling on top of it! Absurd!'

The term grew. Its bewilderments and disasters hardened around me, as if I were being cemented into The Vale.

I now had a bruised familiarity with the typical rhythm of a teaching day. I'd wake feeling, so often, like a condemned man. There'd be the trolleybus journey from my suburb to that inner one. I would read desperately during that journey, stretching myself in the worlds of Gogol, Tolstoy, Hardy . . . It was so huge, the true world, where men wooed and were married, became confident in their characters and labours, underwent immense delights and immense tragedies. I, at The Vale – I, in the company of that girl-gatherer, James, or of Rose-M – was in some impatient antechamber to the real world, the world of mature achievement. When would I be promoted – when would I become an established character, like those with whom I associated in my reading? When would I have weight? When would Britain itself be promoted, become weighty? At the moment, it too seemed to be in some outer chamber, twiddling its thumbs, waiting for peace to become a confident reality . . .

Then junior assembly, with those simple march tunes played on the piano by Mrs Cakebread. As I sat there brooding, sore from the attempt to handle the registration of my own fifteen imps, I could sometimes hardly bear the bouncing jollity of those tunes. It was as if a character from Dostoevsky had got himself mixed up with Disney's seven dwarfs. We'd bounce then into my junior school lessons . . . *Lessons?* Often enough I'd have something carefully prepared, but the moment I entered the classroom my overnight conviction that this was the thing to do would dissolve. I'd intend to teach something about adjectival clauses and instead would find myself giving a spelling test. ('But, sir – you said you'd give us that on Wednesday!') I'd lose all heart in the middle of something prepared, and would suddenly set some foolish little exercise in avoiding the word 'nice'. On one awful occasion I found – virtually as though I'd been taken over by some other person – that I'd directed a class to copy out the first four stanzas of 'The Burial of Sir John Moore'. I'd never in my life consciously intended to require anyone to copy out even a single line of that poem.

I now steadily regarded myself as a destroyer of young minds, hopes and ambitions. What could my little pupils make of my meandering programmes? Their written work seemed desperately careless, and I did not know how to insist that it was decently done. I was not even sure that carefulness was necessary. I was not philosophically sure of that. My own writing, after years of diary-keeping, was crabbed and inscrutable.

Oh, for example there'd been that composition by little Jonathan Honey. Honey's father was a well-known left-wing economist, and I found myself, guiltily, thinking of the little boy's work as if it had been his father's juvenilia. I was rather, and absurdly, in awe of it. In fact, Honey had an unusual view of things, a delight in phrases that gave me great pleasure. He wrote once of being in a room full of music that it was like being inside a piano. He wrote too fast and eagerly to be neat, and sometimes was quite illegible. In the middle of an interesting passage in a composition about his favourite sport – which, he said, was real tennis – a whole phrase could not be deciphered. In the margin I wrote: 'What does this say?' Little Honey later came to my elbow. 'Sir,' he demanded, pointing to my comment. 'What does this say?'

Then, on most days, to the senior school for the second half of the morning. My Upper Five history had become a series of frantic attempts to escape from the medieval monastery. It was clearly not where we should be spending a whole half-term. The form had perfected the most cloying professions of unsatisfied interest in the topic. 'Oh, sir, not Henry VII! He really is *not* one of Nightingale's favourite kings!' 'If you want to please Nightingale, sir, you should let us study some of the queens!' 'Sir, there must be some aspects of the life of a monk that we haven't touched on!' It was a desperate business, trying to steer any kind of course through the rough seas of such comments as these. I'd become greatly confused: calling boys by wrong names – 'I'm not Ransom, sir – *he's* Ransom!' 'Oh no, of course you're not Ransom, are you, Nightingale? Is there a Ransom in the room?' – and transposing words in sentences. The surface of my voice, laid down in the grammar school, began to break up and I dropped my aitches and uttered amazing vowels . . .

Three times a week, misery in the staffroom with Hazard and his aides. Mr Hollow seemed more and more often to be in that inspectorial armchair. After one particularly noisy lesson I'd asked him: 'What does one do with such a class?' and Mr Hollow had said he didn't know. He didn't know what one did with such a class. But Mr Beesley had said: 'They're poor devils, you know – at times I *positively* feel *compassion* for them. They simply aren't bright; nature has *not* been kind. The Common Entrance syllabus is beyond them. I am not at all sure' – and here he paused to give further consideration to the thought in his mind – 'yes, I'm not at all sure that in their circumstances I should not myself be . . . a little *intransigent*.' And Mr Capper, overhearing us, had said: 'Well, yes. One of course positively deplores Nye's existence, but since the . . . creature does exist, one has in the corner of one's mind to admit some feeling of . . . well, *pity*. It's a damned hard row to hoe for our dimmer-witted brethren.' Under the influence of that conversation, I'd gone into a lesson with my tormentors in a mild and missionary mood – ready with the tender smile, the forgiving nod. They were thrown for a moment, and then very quickly realized that the old lame cat had put aside his blunt teeth and whiskers, too. The period ended with appalling denunciations on my part; and on their part, a very special degree of wicked contentment.

Then there was lunch. At The Vale, lunch was not a polite occasion. It had a vulturine quality. Food, an observer might have felt, was being torn here, fiercely ripped by ravenous beaks in a setting of plain uproar. There were eight boys to a table, and a master in charge of each. So it was Mr Beesley's table: Mr Hollow's table: Mr Blishen's table; and each was understood to have its place in a hierarchy of noisiness. Mr Diamond's was the most grave and seemly, and there was thereafter a sharp decline into a loose jocularity which had soon become characteristic of Harrod Parker's, and the plain quality of vocal violence by which my own table was distinguished. I had no positive villains among my boys. In fact, apart from a boy called Cheetham, who was naturally excitable, they were rather dour. But dour noise is quite as bad as any other kind of noise. Even Rider-Smith was noisy. He came from a family of lawyers notable for their puritanical opinions. Little Rider-Smith at eleven had already the air of a man who would later preside over self-constituted committees of inquiry into this or that aspect of our moral decline. Harrod Parker had a special dislike for Rider-Smith. Speaking to the headmaster, he had said: 'The boy's so intolerably smug.'

'Yes, yes,' Mr Juniper had cried, delighted.

'When he's naughty, he's so *piously* naughty!'

'*Ha ha!*'

Mr Juniper's amusement – he sat back in his chair and smiled and nodded his head for a whole minute, and finally raised a hand in salute to Harrod Parker – was a reaction of fully understandable relief. It was impossible not to acknowledge Rider-Smith's sterling qualities, and it was next to impossible not to be made very restive by them.

But at my dinner-table Rider-Smith developed a giggle. It was like being unable to curb the high spirits of a Trappist monk.

And after dinner . . . those crocodiles of boys, to and from the football ground. The untiring chatter of all those shrill voices, all talking at once. The endlessly renewed attempt to keep twenty-two boys in a decent double line, to prevent them from walking backwards and so banging into other pedestrians (always, by some statistical distortion, old ladies), to keep them simply together.

And after that, if I were lucky and wasn't sent to Lower Six, the relatively quiet day's end, with prep . . .

Two afternoons a week, cubbing. Oh, cubbing! I couldn't understand how I'd committed myself to this. At times, bewildered, I found myself teaching the history of the Union Jack. It was not what radicals of my generation would expect themselves to be doing, ever. I carried out this duty with great furtiveness, as if at any moment I might find Kingsley Martin, Harold Laski and John Strachey peering over my shoulder . . .

Some days before we broke up for half-term, Miss Cross, the school secretary, handed me my pay for those stunning six weeks. There was a cheque for £33 3s 8d.

I was cursed with the most damnably unworldly economic outlook. I felt, as I tucked that cheque into my pocket, exactly as I had felt when being paid as a weekly newspaper reporter before the war, and as a landworker during it . . . a sense of very great embarrassment on behalf of my employer. Must he not be rueing the folly of paying out such large sums of money in return for my unimpressive labour?

I felt this even more sharply in respect of my first payment from The Vale. They were getting from me, surely, some kind of anti-labour. I was a positive fraud. How could I blandly take their money? Over my whole existence now hung the nightmarish conviction that I was, in some incurable fashion, unequal to the tasks of teaching. There had been a tremendous heaping up of inadequacies. Wasn't Mr Juniper, even at this moment, waiting for me to dash into his room and throw the cheque down on his desk. 'Sir, I simply cannot take it!' He would say, quietly: 'Well, thank God. For an awful moment or so I'd been afraid that you wouldn't see that this is . . . the only decent thing you can do. Now, I'm sorry. I'm certain there is somewhere an unexacting job that's within your . . . powers. And now – goodbye . . . and let us both thank God that it's over.'

After all, there had been . . . simply my ineptitude in the matter of marks, and ups and downs.

I'd discovered, in the end, what Running-over was. This followed from my discovery of the meaning of 'ups' and 'downs'. If a boy did good work, you put a little bar over the figure in the markbook. That was an up. If he did badly, you put a little bar under the figure, and that was a down.

'Then at Running-over,' I was told by Mr Capper, to whom at

last I had taken my anxious curiosity, 'the Head reads out the number of ups and downs, or both, that a boy has been awarded in each subject. It's very tiresome. I mean, it's tiresome to listen to at Running-over; it's also tiresome to have to enter up in the markbooks.'

I was too appalled to continue the attempt to conceal the full range of my ignorance, 'Then Running-over . . .?'

'God, did no one tell you that? Typical! The Vale never imagines it has to explain itself in respect of any detail of its routine. The Vale's way is the world's way, forsooth! Oh well! Running-over is this fortnightly farrago when parents come and stand in the gallery round the hall and the Head runs over the marks, and calls out the ups and downs.'

'Marks every fortnight?' I cried.

'Marks, places, form orders. Oh, certainly. It would be every week if there weren't some limit to what can be done by flesh and blood. They have to be driven along, the little donkeys, you see, with kicks and carrots, if some of them are to have any hope of getting into decent schools.'

The exhilaration I'd begun to feel, alongside a very great alarm, was pinched out when Mr Capper used that phrase 'decent schools'. I'd thought for a moment that he was a critic of this world of private education, a friend in the enemy's uniform; but his use of that phrase had been entirely without irony. 'Decent' was one of The Vale's keywords. Sometimes, when I heard it used, I thought through faintly appalled inward laughter of the many features of my own existence that would never qualify for it.

'Well, don't worry,' Mr Capper had said. 'Just sit tight and watch what happens next Monday morning. As a matter of fact, tight is what one needs to be, as you'll see. But of course it's much too early in the day for that.'

I *had* worried, of course. I had accumulated, at that time, hardly any marks, and no ups and downs whatever. My conversation with Mr Capper occurred on the very brink of my first Running-over: I had to invent my sets of marks, feeling that my disgrace was now complete. I couldn't bring myself, on that first occasion, to invent also a fort-night's ups and downs. Nothing was ever said about that – but I imagined Mr Juniper being grimly shaken by the discovery that whole forms in whole subjects had perfectly bald marks and placings. I always had difficulty in keeping up the massive supply of marks required to maintain Running-over, but at the beginning I hardly managed it at all. I seemed to find it easy *not* to mark things: or having given marks, to discover that they seemed to bear no relationship to what I saw as true justice between boy and boy. And Running-over was like – oh, worse than any Day of Judgment could be. It was a complex festival of complacency and distress. Mr Juniper peppered it with extempore comment. It was another consequence of his having been a headmaster so long. He was full of judgments. Many of these were perfectly kind. But he might say: 'Evans i – are you ever going to have half the brains of your little brother?' Or: 'Buchman – a down in Geography! – you should eat less, Buchman! Too much food makes you dull!' And though jokes about being less brainy than a brother, or being too fat, might give some boys a sense of being *characters*, of having a place made for them in the community – to others, I guessed, they would make Running-over, already an ordeal, virtually unbearable.

But it *was*, I could see, part of the whole of that ambitious pattern of private education. Many boys at The Vale flew high. For the kind of flight they were launched upon, such endless occasions of praise and blame were clearly considered vital.

I was simply glad, but rather incredulous, that the records of the staff were exempt from assessment and public announcement at Running-over. Huge quantities of downs would hardly have expressed my own disgrace.

With Rose-M, too, it was all ups and downs. Somewhere I'd read that one should 'range one's sexual instincts behind one's character and affections'. I saw the beautiful sense of that; but, my goodness, there were in my case more elements than these to attempt to draft into orderly ranks. 'Get into line,' I might for instance have been crying, 'my social and political outlooks!' I did not flinch, in my dreadful social nerviness, only from the fact that the house she lived in had a name and not a number. (In my world, to give your house a name was regarded as a piece of laughable pretension.) I was distressed not only by her having a telephone. I was also ready to be taken aback by the clothes she wore. On one chilly late-autumn night, she came to The Under Thirties, an opulent ball of golden fur. Among the thoughts that filled my cringing mind was that I'd simply never be the sort of man able to maintain a lifelong supply of such coats.

So often, when we were walking side by side through the town, I was filled with an excitement that seemed very close to simple happiness. For days I was haunted by the memory of her face turned up to mine in the light of a street lamp – it had glowed with coloured mischief, a promise of . . . teasing affection. Then I felt the most powerful desire to believe there was no fatal gulf between us. I saw no sense, then in the thoughts that woke me sharply in the night: that these excitements had the slenderest foundations: that it was easily possible to imagine, beyond this experience, a truly wholehearted sort of wooing: that I was perhaps only one in a string of men with whom Rose-M played . . . warm games: that we'd never once exchanged a friendly, honest confidence. Flippancy had set the tone of so many of our conversations.

63

I'd been coming back from football with Mrs Cakebread, one afternoon, and suddenly had caught sight of Rose-M and her mother, walking towards us. They'd clearly been shopping. I was carrying the coloured ribbons the boys wore to distinguish one team from the other. Blossom ii had one of my hands tight in his. I felt like a mixture of nursemaid and policeman. To Mrs Cakebread's surprise, I dashed us all, rather dangerously, across the nearest, extremely unsuitable crossing.

'I saw you,' said Rose-M when we next met.

'I know,' I said miserably. 'With those ribbon things in my hands.'

'Oh,' said Rose-M. 'I didn't notice. I thought you looked sad. That's all. I wish you didn't so often look sad. When you're walking with me for example, good sir! It isn't very flattering, a girl might think. !

'Oh no,' I said. 'I mean, I don't— What I mean is, I didn't know I looked sad the other afternoon, but if I did it was because of football.'

'But why should you be sad about football? It seems an odd thing to be sad about.'

'Football and love. Sad matters,' I declared wildly.

'You are a disheartening chap, really! Do say something cheerful, for a change. I know you can, when you try.'

Oh yes, there were funny things I wanted to tell her. Things I found funny. Of my discovery, for example, that the worst class could be charmed into silence with a story. I read so many now, in odd periods in the afternoon. I was reading *Emil and the Detectives* to one of the younger classes in the junior school. They were so smitten with it that, to Miss Seakins's mild dismay (the junior school was kept by its very competent ladies in an orderly state that reminded me, for some reason, of well-made beds), they would rush down from their upper landing to a lower one, to take me, as I came in, under their brisk and breathless control. They'd surround me and fairly drag and shove me up the stairs. 'Come on, sir. You're late!' (There were perhaps thirty seconds involved.) 'He'd fallen asleep. In the train with the man with the bowler hat. Quick!' I'd be ushered into their room and thrust into my chair and they'd glare at any boy who, with some accidental fidgeting, threatened a further delay. 'Come *on*, sir!' And then . . . their beautiful attention! My voice, unaccustomed to these long stints of reading aloud, growing rougher and rougher – my whole system, under the strain, threatening to lapse into sleep. There was a tiny boy in that class who was obdurately of the belief that I was called 'Mr Magician'. 'Thank you,' he took it upon himself to say as each reading ended amid groans, sighs and passionate attempts to swear me to perfect future punctuality, 'thank you, Mr Magician!'

Their form mistress was so striking in appearance that people had fallen into the habit of referring to her as 'the lovely Miss Jones';

and this had somehow become her name, exactly as if it had been written in that form on her birth certificate. Even very small boys spoke formally of 'the lovely Miss Jones'. One afternoon when I'd come over to read *Emil*, she'd hung on to her class, attempting to discover the boy responsible for a small disturbance of the kind that in the junior school passed for a quite serious crime. When at last I was admitted to the room, the class surrounded me with angry cries. 'Sir, it was the lovely Miss Jones!' 'Sir, you ought to report the lovely Miss Jones to Miss Seakins!' 'Sir, the lovely Miss Jones is the most horrid teacher we've ever had!'

Away from Rose-M, I rehearsed such stories for her ear. Why then, when we met, did I not tell them? Why did they seem, somehow, inapt – even when her company gave me this sense of excitement that might, for all I could tell, be a quality of real happiness?

I wanted to tell her sad things, too. Odd sadnesses – such as the moment when Mr Juniper, at assembly, spoke of the execution, the night before, of the Nazi leaders. 'These wicked men,' said Mr Juniper, 'have paid the penalty for their evil actions.' And two hundred small boys clapped . . . and cheered. It seemed oddly horrible that this final act in the European Grand Guignol should have been made the occasion of this innocent applause, which would have been just as enthusiastic for the result of a school victory in football.

But instead of such exchanges between Rose-M and me . . . those rallies of flippancy! It was wrong, it was wrong. But then she smiled at me, and once more I found it impossible to accept the judgment of common sense. I was lonely, I was full of long-starved desire – these were the unsound roots of my readiness to play . . . whatever game it was we were playing. That is what common sense told me. But it seemed to speak in such a mean voice, if I thought of her smiles . . .

I had never in my life shaved so often, with such care, or brushed my hair with such a hope of producing some effect of . . . burnishing.

All day before one of our meetings I'd be in a state of vastly over-excited anticipation. A kind of languor would be added to the sleepiness that threatened me as I read to those intent little boys of Middle Two. How did I get into such a state? I wondered.

After one meeting, I was certain I'd set my ideas at last on a stable foundation. Rose-M, I briskly told myself, had the bloom and colour of youth, and by this I was perfectly naturally drawn. I enjoyed teasing her. She wasn't remarkably bright – had no intellectual edge – and there was certainly something missing: a depth of understanding I needed if I were to be happily in love. I would hurt her, too, by being always ill-at-ease in her world of lively surfaces. She lacked an exploring imagination. Oh, she wanted life to be kept small and bright and dependable, and I wanted to open it up, and to be at risk. Something of the sort.

Ah, that was better. Here was quiet objectivity at work. All was well.

And our next meeting filled me with the strangest fear. Now she seemed . . . so tender and sweet. She wore a dress that revealed slim white shoulders. I was filled, the whole evening, with an aching desire to be gentle and affectionate. How easily I could surrender to my giddy desire to be in love! And what would be the outcome? What had Rose-M and I in common? What durable satisfaction could either offer to the other?

I was suddenly afraid that this feeling of immense tenderness would be too strong for me . . .

The next day was the last of my first half-term at The Vale. During the morning Mr Juniper summoned me to his room. 'I think,' he said, 'that next term I shall bring you over to the senior school for most of the time. I think it's been very good of you to teach those little ones. It's good for them to have a man, now and then. But I think you may find it more satisfying to spend more time over here.'

I realized this was a vote of confidence, but could not imagine the grounds for it. The facts were simple. I'd overshot my mark. I was engaged in a dangerous deception, and my basic desire was to scream and run away. Mr Juniper's words made things worse, if anything. The exposure, when it came, would be all the more shameful.

Looking through newspapers, now, I'd found myself searching for news of a schoolmaster in trouble. I'd be eased if I discovered such a story. It wouldn't be so awful, I wouldn't be so lonely in my knowledge of secret imposture, if I could assure myself that, somewhere, some other teacher had been less than perfect.

My last lesson of the half-term was with the full Middle Four. Their acts of indiscipline were multitudinous. I gave what could only be described as a virtuoso solo performance on the instrument of amazed wrath. I found myself waiting for them to build up to a peak of inattentive noisiness: then I would, as it were, take the whole spectacle in my hands, confront it with incredulous indignation, and burst into a rage.

'I don't know why you go to the expense of coming here just to make noise,' I said. They rolled about, almost affectionately enjoying this comic statement.

At last, close to indifference, I told them to clear their desks and sit upright: we'd spend the last ten minutes of the period in silence. The room filled with ill-suppressed gigglings. Rider-Smith was having particular difficulty in keeping laughter at bay. 'Oh, laugh if you want to, Rider-Smith: don't hold it back,' I advised him – myself driven by an odd kind of near-affection. The giggles burst out of him, then, and the entire class exploded . . .

That evening, Rose-M and I exchanged declarations of love.

Part Two

I

An extremely small boy clutched my hand as I made my way to
school and scurried along beside me. My other hand had for some
minutes been in the possession of a boy who'd not opened his mouth.
'Sir,' said the newcomer. 'Do you know the story about Thomas
Tobacco?'

'Thomas Tobacco? Who was he?'

'He was the Arch – He was – The King said "Who will rid me
of this – ?" They killed him with their swords. In the— *you know*.'

'Ah – Thomas à Becket!'

'The lovely Miss Jones told us that story.'

'Much in the prep school world,' my friendly adviser had told me,
'has a fragile charm. I think you must beware of being seduced by it.'

Oh, seduction by it was not too likely, I felt. Going home the
previous evening I'd shared the top of the bus with half a dozen of
the little creatures. They'd crowded round me. 'Sir – where do you
live? – in a lunatic asylum?' 'Sir – where do you live? – in a lavatory?'
And as they clattered together down the stairs, having reached their
stop, they called up a rhythmical series of injunctions. 'Goodnight
sir! Don't forget to have a bath tonight!' 'Don't forget to wash your
hair, sir!' 'Don't forget to wash your ears, sir!' The bus, once their
shrill excitements had been left behind, felt as solemn as . . . Canter-
bury Cathedral itself. I'd smiled through it all – it must have looked
hideous, a fixed smile of desperate tolerance – and the bus was full
of stares, incredulous grins.

That was less than seductive. And oh God, I ought surely – in all
decency I *ought* to resign!

And yet an accumulation of habits, of repetitions – even of repeated
agonies and disasters – had made me feel that I was actually drawing
a little away from the hopelessness of my first responses to teaching
at The Vale.

There'd been, early in that second half-term, a number of small
occurrences – oh, the tiniest of events – that had helped me towards

this very cautious feeling of being rather more at home. The first had begun with the interruption of a lesson I was uneasily conducting in an attic classroom. Mr Capper, responsible for Middle Six English, was down with the flu, and I'd become his substitute. It would have saved misunderstanding and wasted effort if Mr Juniper had said, frankly: 'Oh, just go up there and let them amuse themselves at your expense.' These were bigger, brighter boys than I'd so far taught, and I was fairly frightened by the way their misconduct seemed to arise without a blameable source. My discomfort was the greater because in the class was the son of a novelist who'd long been one of my heroes. I felt as if I were, not even at one remove, under the scornful eye of the father. I was ashamed of being, under that gaze, so crude and clumsy and uninspired; and I was ashamed of my shame . . .

Mr Juniper wanted me at once in his room. I dissuaded Middle Six from providing me with a mock-solicitous escort ('Hard luck, sir!') and went down to the study where the headmaster was accustomed to sit briefly between his impatient forays through the school. He said: 'Ah, would you like extra classes?'

'You mean—?'

'There are nine boys in Lower Six who are not far away from Common Entrance, and Mr Beesley says they can't spell or punctuate – in short, they are illiterate. You would take them twice a week – for half an hour . . .'

Mr Juniper then began to think, financially, aloud. The regular rate for extra lessons was 7s 6d an hour. If I took them, say, on Tuesdays and Thursdays, then nine times . . .

It was too difficult for The Vale's remedial maths master. I quickly lost touch with Mr Juniper's analysis. Such calculations as I was able to make I kept to myself; and they had reference to my hopes of meeting Rose-M, and the part that such extra teaching might play in preventing or delaying such meetings. I could not tell Mr Juniper that I was, at the moment, qualified only to teach the nervous arithmetic of love.

I left the room not much worried by my failure to follow his reasoning or make much of his instructions. I'd already discovered that only a small fraction of Mr Juniper's ideas and impulses ever led to action. He needed, himself, the constant spur that came from feeling that he was interfering creatively in the running of the school. Mr Beesley, I guessed, had made some small polite noise about misplaced commas, and this had been expanded at once into a massive breakdown of literacy. To Mr Juniper, we were always in the midst of battle. There'd be this stream of urgent, sometimes haggard, instructions from the bridge. Old hands, who knew that most of the time we were drifting along nicely in home waters, would look awfully alert, salute briskly, and carry on as before.

But somehow, being however implausibly asked to give extra lessons made me feel I belonged – I was edging my way into the picture. And this feeling was almost at once strengthened by a staffroom discussion in which I found my views on teaching being warmly approved by – of all people – Mr Diamond and Mr Hollow.

Of these two senior men I was particularly in awe. I believed they must have formed the most savage opinion of my usefulness. Here was I, bleating and ineptly roaring my way through the school day, and getting nowhere. Here were they: among other things, effective masters of the long-standing teacher's instant apoplexy.

With Mr Hollow this was often sparked off by lunch – the only sphere in which, so far as I could make out, he was in fact a little less than totally competent. A large man, he was driven by the fear that he'd be cheated of his due share of a dish. Many boys at The Vale were vegetarian; and alternative lunches, for them and the meat-eaters, were served every day. These meals were always first-class; The Vale had, for a school, astonishingly subtle kitchens. From day to day the slight edge of excellence was to be found now in the meat dish, now in the other. Masters tended to change their dietary principles from lunch to lunch. It was the custom for them, on a fairly informal rota, to do the serving. Each table sent up a boy to collect the dishes: so there was a constant buzzing queue at the serving table, much jostling and thrusting of plates, and some merriment with ladles when lighter-hearted members of staff were using them. Mr Hollow was the only master who constituted himself a server day after day, with never a break. He would serve at first in silence, with a busy contained fury behind which, you sensed, lay his fierce hunger; and then, as the amounts of food dwindled, his fury spilled over and found a voice. It found, of course, his own rather special voice; but indeed his habitual obscurity of speech, at this juncture, became worse than usual. He'd suspect that gluttony was at work in all directions, that unlicensed servers were making off with second and even third helpings. His ladle would begin to flash out at the remaining boys, like a clumsy rapier. Indeed, at times it was treated as such, and briefly there'd be the spectacle of Mr Hollow's indignant serving spoon being subjected to thrust and parry by a fork snatched up by, say, my enemy Hazard. 'B'n bef' ', Mr Hollow would seem roughly to be roaring. 'Dam' greed! M' boys than sch'l has. 'Snuff! S'n y' bef', 'n I?'

What appeared to move both Mr Hollow and Mr Diamond was a tremendous impatience with the young. Mr Hollow indeed was quite racked with a sort of general impatience. He'd pace up and down in the staffroom, working up his indignation at the complexities of the Vale day. 'L'k here,' he'd bark, suddenly halting in front of a colleague. 'L'k here! Can take Up' Three prep?' 'But of course,' was the usual mild reply. 'Abs'lutel' un'void'le,' Mr Hollow would shout. 'See, 'f Raisin takes Low' Six, th'n—' His explanation would peter out in a glaring smile. 'But of course.' Impossible not to feel, with Mr Hollow's face a few stormy inches from one's own, a kind of crazy guilt. One must oneself be responsible for his anguish! 'Good 'f you,' Mr Hollow would groan: and move on to the next interview in his desperate pattern of encounters, out of whose moans and sawn-off explanations would at last emerge the usual bland shape of our afternoons. We'd leave Mr Hollow grinding his teeth in the staffroom, pacing up and down, shaking his head over the enormity of it all.

Mr Diamond's wrath was a little different. It alternated with bluff good humour, and did so without an intervening mood. He would turn enormously red and begin to move about the place with immense strides. 'My goodness, my goodness,' he'd growl. He'd be smiling at lunch, and a second later would leap to his feet, red with rage, and clap his hands for attention. I've never known anyone so able to command silence, where a moment before had been great noise, by a mere clapping of hands. They were large and resonant hands. The school had taught itself, nervously, to hear and heed them in almost any circumstances. 'My goodness, my goodness,' he'd roar, leaping on to a chair: sometimes from that to a table top. 'Where are we, then? A bear garden, is that where we are?' Sometimes we were invited to say whether we were in a circus, or at a football match, or on Hampstead Heath on a Bank Holiday. 'Is that where we are, Hazard – Hussar – what's your name, laddie? – Is that where we are, the boy with the red hair? I'm sorry, Mr B. Not you. The boy behind you. Well, boy, make up your mind. Is your hair red or not? Eh? Speak up, lad!' All the boys in the area concerned, amazed by this sudden turn of events, which introduced the notion that to be uncertain of the colour of your hair was an offence, and might indeed be the very crime that had caused Mr Diamond to leap on to chair or table and clap those terrifying hands – all these boys would consult one another in a panic as to their being red-haired or not. 'What's all the jabbering about, then? Fuller, is that Fuller? what are you *gassing* about, laddie?' 'Gassing' was one of Mr Diamond's favourite words. It referred to an offence of wide, vague character. Even some forms of silence were denounced as 'gassing'. For it, whatever it might turn out to be, Mr Diamond reserved some of his most oppressive punishments. Together with his failure to be accurate in calling out names, this other vagueness led to the formation, in the hall, of tremendous whirlpools of pure confused terror, efforts at self-exculpation, even muttered attempts to shift the mysterious blame to other shoulders. As often as not Mr Diamond's wrath would die away as quickly as it had come. 'Well, then!' he'd roar, and glare at us all, and clamber down to resume his perfectly jocular lunch. There'd be, for a whole minute or so, a baffled silence, during which it seemed that everyone present was trying to isolate himself from his companions – to look, in general, as if he weren't there at all: or, if there, then silently, circumspectly alone. Then, beginning with an exploratory whispering, the noise would mount once more.

I had nightmares of being punished, in some huge unspecific fashion, by Mr Diamond and Mr Hollow together, for the slackness and general wretched character of my teaching.

But here I was, early in that second half-term, talking to Harrod Parker in the staffroom about the merits of certain kinds of parrot-like learning at an early age. Mr Diamond turned out to have been listening. He actually leapt to his feet and took up his place at my side, as if I'd raised a standard that he, for one, must flock to. 'My goodness, yes! My goodness, young man, how true that is! As practical men, we know it must be done.'

That phrase about being practical was a favourite with Mr Diamond. He used it as though throughout life he'd been the victim of a conspiracy to convict him of airily theoretical approaches to things. I was myself at this time deeply opposed to the idea of being practical, in any way whatever. There was a cluster of words that were devious ways of saying 'conservative'; and 'practical' was one of them. But I felt marvellously flattered by Mr Diamond's readiness to admit me to his club, even under such a heading.

'Oh, it must indeed be done,' I said. 'Better a little light-hearted misery at seven or eight than much real misery at a less flexible age.'

'I don't think it's even misery,' said Harrod Parker. 'They enjoy it. Acquiring useful knowledge by hammering it into your head with constant rhythmical repetition – oh, for a small fellow, very enjoyable!'

'Take,' I said, quite carried away, 'my maths division of Middle Four – you know, the lot I have here in the staffroom three times a week . . . Part of their trouble is that in the juniors they were taught by a temporary wartime teacher – so Miss Seakins tells me – who believed that you learned your multiplication tables best by a process she called "absorption".'

'Good heavens,' cried Mr Diamond, ready to be apoplectic without hearing another word.

'The tables,' I said, 'were written out and hung round the room, and the idea was that the boys would absorb them just as they absorbed air, unconsciously.'

'Great Scott,' cried Mr Diamond. 'My hat!' He laughed in a rather broken fashion. 'You know, the war was a disaster in more ways than one . . . !'

At this point Mr Hollow intervened. Interested, he said, to hear talk of that division of Middle Four. In his view, a great mistake.

'Oh, indeed,' I cried eagerly. 'They're the worst boys in the form and they positively enjoy being singled out and put together. They feel they're in quite glorious disgrace. They act upon one another.'

'Act 'pon 'noth'', Mr Hollow echoed, warmly. And apart from that, he said, it really wasn't fair on the man who had to teach them. It was a most unfortunate introduction to maths teaching, and he was very sorry about it. Look – would I like him to speak to Mr Juniper?

'Not,' I said anxiously, 'giving him the idea that I'm bending under the strain.'

No, no. It wasn't my suggestion. It was his. He did feel it was damned unfair to me. Mr Hollow then gave me one of his smiles – those overwrought, glaring smiles – and I felt suddenly ashamed. I'd thought of him as a species of enemy – hostile to my teaching, a rather angry, brusque man. But his concern was clearly genuine. And surely there was . . . more smile than glare?

I was positively in the club, now. One of my opinions on teaching (did I really hold it?) had been acclaimed, I had been commiserated with as a victim of Mr Juniper's impulsive rearrangements of the timetable.

The third incongruous step towards the increasing of my confidence followed almost at once, and resulted from yet another of Mr Juniper's seizures of decision. He bustled up to me during a break in the senior school. 'This is for you,' he cried, taking me by a sleeve. Absent-mindedly he imparted a small correction to the angle of my spine. Himself, for all his age, a man of great spryness, bright with health, he equated youth with total hardihood. He tutted if he saw me wearing an overcoat. As I discovered later, a young member of his staff purporting to have a cold was an almost incredible omen of approaching deca-dence. Coming up behind me, he'd seize my shoulders and press them back. 'Stand up straight – *always*! Give your chest a chance!' Now he hastily remoulded my torso, saying as he did this: 'The boys want to form an aeromodel club. You're of the generation that understands these things. You know all about aeromodels. There's a meeting on now. Come along.' I looked round at my colleagues, desperately, and saw no help in their grins. I had made my last model of any kind – oh, it must have been fifteen years before: one of those cardboard things, stick tab A to tab B; and my sad constructs had never lasted more than half an hour. I hurried miserably in Mr Juniper's wake and feared the worst as we entered the bellroom and I saw twenty or so senior faces turned in our direction. 'Here,' cried Mr Juniper, 'is your President. Ah, Ross-Stinson minor, this is your brainchild, isn't it? How's your father? Oh, and do something about that little brother of yours, won't you? Miss Seakins tells me he's been asleep solidly for six months . . . Come on, someone! A chair for your President! You couldn't have a better man for the task. A thoroughly modern young man – knows all about it . . . Carry on then, Mr Blishen.'

And they were eager. They were polite. I seemed to know what to do: referring sympathetically to the project, hastily appointing a secretary and treasurer, proposing certain initial tasks, dividing those present into the experienced and the beginners.

My reward I reaped at once . . . Boys, with incredibly grave faces, pursued me along corridors, politely halted me on staircases. 'Sir, I've been thinking—' 'Sir, I wonder if you'd agree—?'

The gravity and earnestness of their manner brought me . . . oh, dammit, close to tears. I felt I'd had the most dramatic intimation of the remote possibility that, if I stayed long enough at The Vale and worked away at a total transformation of my character – and took, perhaps, a brilliant external degree – and if I had Rose-M to support me, herself transformed into some sort of studious domestic aide . . . then I might become a teacher, after all.

2

I was now possessed by the belief that Rose-M and I must marry. My old calculations in the matter had been left far behind; I despised them.

On the day we broke up for half-term, there'd been a meeting of The Under Thirties. Afterwards, I stood with Rose-M at one elbow; and at the other, James, who'd been set seething by the evening's entertainment – a recital of gramophone records. A Haydn symphony (one reelingly gathered) had caused James to form a theory that might well lead to the overthrow of a massive amount of musicological dogma. 'You see . . .' he was saying, when Rose-M murmured: 'I think *Evelyn* would be *fascinated* by this.'

'Oh – yes, I'm sure,' said James, and went at once across the room to lower the burden of this notion of his on to the frail shoulders of the group's secretary – a pretty girl, whom of late he seemed persuaded that he could subdue to his desires by treating her in this fashion: as, that is, a sort of intellectual pack-mule. Rose-M touched my arm. 'A good moment,' she whispered, 'to step into the night.' 'But James—' I said; and then followed her.

Damn James, I suddenly found myself thinking: and damn all loyalty to friends. Damn all logic, consequence, good sense. Damn all bothered calculations. Damn everything but that haze of warmth, scentedness, sparkle, promise of softness and infinitely stimulating motion, that was now at my side . . . The strange magic that had accumulated over recent days was running loose. My heart leapt, fluttered, danced. There was a sudden space in my stomach; I was empty, yearning, full of every variety of hunger. I told her as we passed the old grammar school how I'd run through its gates sixteen years earlier, one of the town boys sent, with brand-new rulers, virgin blotting paper, new penholders and nibs, to take the scholarship. I'd felt sick that day with excitement and dread and bewilderment. What *was* the grammar school? It was cruel, certainly – I'd had no doubt about that. There was the Tudor rose in stone set in the worn brickwork of each of the gateposts: and that frightful date in the sixteenth century, the year of the school's founding. There was the hall where we sat for the exam, which had been the original school: with its four corner towers, the red post rising in the middle of it that was whispered of as 'the whipping post'. To my ten-year-old mind it all fused with what I'd learned of Tudor history: a matter of beheadings, largely. To me, taking the scholarship was very close to an appointment on Tower Hill . . .

Rose-M said she could see me, running through the gates. And where was she at the time? I asked. Oh, they were living in Sweden. Yes, in 1930 – Sweden. Her father was representing his firm in Stockholm. She was a child of six, then, and remembered chiefly losing her fur gloves, and weeping . . .

Oh, I said, unable to bear the thought of those tears. Oh, she said – to think of that little boy running scared between those gateposts . . .

Oh, said our hands, and flew together, and clung with desperate tightness. And we walked on for a minute or so, unable, for trembling and amazement – for this sense of being in the grip of the strangest sweet force – to turn and face each other.

Then Rose-M said: 'Oh, I thought you never would.'

'It was obvious?'

'I know lots of men not half as nice who'd have thought it was.'

'Oh, please – I'm not nice.'

'You would like not to be, wouldn't you! That's why I— one of the reasons why I—'

A kiss that was drowning – was falling singing over a cliff.

I had to break away to blow my nose. 'You never see this in films,' I said. 'Never in films do they interrupt a kiss to blow their noses.'

'*Films!*' murmured Rose-M, as if I'd made reference to some adorable absurdity.

That great emptiness inside me had been filled with incredulity. Me? Why should this delightful girl conceive a liking for a clumsy monster like me? And I was afraid, too. Suddenly she, a comparative stranger, had become the most intimate of persons. The fusion of these extremes of relationship made me frightened, dizzy . . .

Later we were in the kitchen of her house, talking in whispers. She was making plans for us. During a break in dancing, she was earning pocket money by looking after a family of small children. I was to come and fetch her from work, next day. 'I shall feel,' I said, 'like a guardsman. I shall have to wait while you take your apron and cap off, and take your leave of your mistress.'

She was kneeling on the floor, her head in my lap. An enormous blissful fatigue possessed us. I thought it might make sense never to stir again. Any movement must bring about a decline of our condition.

And suddenly, again, a sense of myself as the clumsy monster. Oh, that tangle of feelings that waited on the edge of this perfect moment! How heavy they made me! Must she not suddenly look up at me and be disenchanted and send me away?

This delicate and sensitive thing, a woman! I said something awkward, forgetting instantly what it was I'd said, aware only of a terrible fear . . . until she lifted her head from my lap and was smiling . . .

I walked home thinking that all I'd told myself about Rose-M was idiocy, the speculations of a scoundrel whose skin I'd surely sloughed. Now all would be different.

The next day, until I met her, had been one of almost unbearable restlessness. I distrusted myself so terribly. Could I hope to keep at bay my self-suspicion, my readiness to imagine that women were devious and deceitful? The first of these feelings told me that Rose-M couldn't care for such a person: the second built upon that, insistent that Rose-M's motives must be complex, shifting . . . even sinister.

But I went to meet her happily. Our hands would fly together again – there would be that unconsidered certainty of action, of union. Something better than my broodings would be in charge.

Such an astonishment to see her, running up the road towards me – smaller than I'd thought: startlingly real, altogether. I'd disappointed her, by not precisely coming to the house. Her employer had said: 'Where then is this young man who was calling for you?' 'Oh I never thought—', I said. 'I never imagined – *knocking*!'

'Nothing terrible about knocking at a door,' said Rose-M, and took command of my hand.

But oh, instant heaviness! My mind became a clot of dull metal. Her quick, excited words, the tenderness of her touch, her rallyings – in exchange for these I offered dullness. Suddenly I did not know how to be the man who could give her a fit return for the gift of her love.

A few days before, I thought, I'd been computing what she had to offer me. Now I scanned my dull nature and could find in it nothing to offer to her.

At her front gate she said: 'Come in.' I shook my head dumbly. 'Remember – I'm going away for a few days— Can't you? . . . All right, then. Edward, be cheerful! We've got . . . so much to be cheerful about, haven't we? I shall miss your . . . sad face so much! The moment I'm back you ring me – remember. *The moment I'm back!*'

I seemed to be all heart, and all that heart aching. Did she not seek the very things I could not provide – fun, gaiety, affection, fused into the lightest, springiest certainty? Instant, spontaneous acceptance of things? Across my mind's eye passed a procession of men who might make worthy husbands for her. They were men amazingly charming and interesting. They were not, as I was, futureless – without the least scrap of ordinary talent for contriving some sort of prospects. They were not engaged in farcically ill-paid impostures as ushers in private schools.

We would marry. Rose-M had said so. There had been a moment, that first evening of declared love, that was like the signing of a treaty of marriage. Rose-M had even laid out a draft plan of procreation. We would marry, surely. She was offering herself, all her brightness . . .

I was deeply terrified by the suspicion that I'd lack the simple efficiency to take up that offer.

Incorrigibly I failed to look to my future. There'd been a teacher of mine, at the grammar school, over whose most casual utterances I'd been given to thinking deeply, often guiltily. He'd never made me so uneasy as when he said – I think about some utterly trivial matter – 'The wise man, you know, anticipates the course of nature.' I anticipated nothing, but dragged at nature's erratic heels, persistently. I rather despised those calculations that my fellows devoted to their careers, to their future selves. James at twenty-six was very preoccupied with the comfort of James at forty.

Well, my future was bound up, I supposed, with that promise I'd made to Mr Juniper: to seek professional qualifications as a teacher. I had two vague intentions. One was to take an external degree, in something, somewhere. I was not in fact certain that I'd be permitted to embark on a degree course. Had I ever matriculated? Did my School Certificate (five passes, I seemed to remember) amount to an exemption from matriculation? For an answer to that question, I'd have to send my Certificate to the university. But first I'd need to track down the Certificate, which had vanished.

My second intention was to seek admission to the emergency training scheme. I'd already reapplied, and had heard nothing. To my dismay, I felt perfectly comfortable about the Ministry's strict silence. I should be agitated, should I not? I should be writing letters of sharp inquiry, if not of admonition? But I drifted on, mesmerized by nature's wayward heels . . .

At times I asked myself – with small hope of answer – such questions as: How long did I wish to be a servant of this charming but arbitrary branch of education?

Mr Diamond said: 'Of course, the kind of boys who come here has changed. In the old days they were from the best families in the neighbourhood. But the district's quite different now. Oh, character completely gone! Ah, yes! No feeling for The Vale! No *esprit de corps*!'

I remembered an ex-soldier who'd been one of our foremen on the land. Joe had claimed to be bitterly regretful because landwork exhibited, in his phrase, no S.P.D. Cor.

'S.P.D. Cor?' we'd asked him, wonderingly.

'S.P.D. Cor, mates – what you've never heard of! Pride in the regiment, you grinning apes!'

Part of that collapse of the social dignity of the district that Mr Diamond spoke of was attributed, in much staffroom talk, to the insidious spread of socialism. Some of the most distinguished exponents of this alien doctrine even sent their sons to The Vale. But it was widely felt among my colleagues that the results of the 1945 election were inexplicable – perhaps (it might be discovered if only one could get the thing properly looked into) the product of a simple if fantastic piece of miscounting.

Mr Raisin put it bluntly once, over a staffroom tea. 'One has never,' he said, 'seen a motor accident, has one? So curious, that! Just as one never seems to meet anyone who voted Labour.'

I opened my mouth, quite miserably. It would serve no useful purpose to inform Mr Raisin that I had myself voted in that extra-ordinary fashion. The news would merely perplex him. He liked me, I knew, and would be unable to absorb the notion that a young man capable of capping a quotation from Milton might be politically rotten. But it had to be said. And so it would have been, if Mrs Plenty had not spoken first.

Mrs Plenty was Senior School Art, part-time. She took, very coolly, the brunt of Mr Juniper's views on Art, as currently taught. These views, deeply disgruntled ones, he expressed from time to time at morning prayers. Harrod Parker and I had found that we both expected him any day now to incorporate his discontents in the prayers themselves. 'Oh Lord,' he would urge that most senior of headmasters, 'please do something about Mrs Plenty's use of paper.' 'Paper,' he would in fact inform the assembled senior school when his irascibility ran away with him, 'costs goodness knows what a ream or packet or whatever one buys it in – and you'd be startled by the bills! The bills are frankly startling! But there it is, or there it seems to be! – there's this very odd idea that boys can be taught to paint only by being allowed *enormous* sheets of paper, and by being encouraged to – *ha!*' At such a point as this Mr Juniper's wrath would master him, and he would beat the table in front of him and make huge shapes in the air with his hands in an attempt to convey to the inattentive school the pointlessness of the kind of painting in which they were encouraged. 'Well, we can only say,' he'd conclude, typically sharing his ownership of the opinion with us all, 'that we wonder whether Picasso or Matisse can *draw* as well as Leonardo da Vinci.'

These treacheries were not uttered in the actual presence of his Art mistress: being a part-timer, Mrs Plenty never attended prayers. But had she been sitting by his side, Mr Juniper would certainly not have refrained from cheerfully undermining her authority. The free expression of impatient opinions was natural to him. There had been an occasion when a party of footballers had returned to school, one short. The missing boy was the son of a major civil servant. 'Great Scott!' Mr Juniper had cried, standing on the balcony overlooking the senior hall and addressing indiscriminately such staff and pupils as might be within earshot. 'This is a very important boy! The last boy we can afford to lose like this! Find him at once, someone. Look everywhere, and keep me informed!' Had it made sense to suggest that we lose two boys of less importance in return for the restoration of this one, I'm sure Mr Juniper would have proposed it. 'Take Smith B. J. and Bugden-Thomas,' he would have called, 'and abandon them somewhere. Hurry! Hurry!'

Mrs Plenty, face to face with any rumour of Mr Juniper's views on Art, or receiving an apoplectic hint from the Head himself, would usually powder her nose. She had an untidy face, large, its elements thrown together, as if she reassembled them each morning hurriedly and rather inexactly. It was as if, in terms of physiognomy, her slip was always showing, her shoulder straps always displaced. This was what was true of her actual clothes. She was an unselfconscious affront to the elegance of the staffroom. In the matter of using powder, she seemed to be trying, but not too earnestly, to compose herself for the conventional gaze. So she'd hurl powder over the pleasant disorder of her features, as if that might help her to pass through the world of The Vale without being too much goggled at. Perhaps it was the same instinct that often led her to pull her stockings tight. She would raise the hem of her skirt and there'd be an explosion of elastic, quite out of tune with the characteristic sounds of the staffroom: those neat witty voices, the clearings of throats, the methodical laughter. I remember the first time this happened – the raising of the skirt, the noise of private snapping . . . It had been under Mr Raisin's eye: he'd been in mid-quotation – from Milton, of course: he'd halted, as if he too had been snapped, but too vehemently, so that some inner elastic had parted. He'd stared, incredulous. Mrs Plenty had then taken out the considerable quantity of apparatus with which she did her powdering, and sought to expunge her face. 'I can understand anyone forgetting a line written by that bloody Milton,' she'd said, consoling him.

Now, at this other occasion over the staffroom tea, and as Mr Raisin looked round at us to collect our assents to his theory of the absolute invisibility of Labour voters, Mrs Plenty said: 'Well, I voted Labour; and shall do so again.' Elastic snapped, powder flew.

Said Mr Raisin, after an enormous pause: 'But since these fellows came in—'

'And I think they're doing rather well, in difficult circumstances,' said Mrs Plenty, cheerfully.

'But—'

Mrs Plenty seemed about to offer her powder puff to her incredulous colleague. 'What don't you like about them?' she asked. A mother of four – her house, we gathered, always full of stray children, a great sluttishness of children – Mrs Plenty seemed to be drawing upon her experience in that field in dealing with Mr Raisin. I saw suddenly that she must have regarded the whole of the Vale staff as a gathering of irrational little conservative children, given to the utterance of silly but often quite droll opinions. 'What have they done wrong?' she insisted.

'Well,' said Mr Raisin, speaking as though from within a noose. 'Since these fellows got in, the country has ceased to be great. That's all. The governments of the past made Britain great. That's the point, isn't it? And these fellows are dismantling it all, you see. That's it.'

He had risen and was making his way to the door, his intention clear: not to go anywhere in particular, but simply to go. His hand on the doorknob, he looked back and, with a faint effect of reanimation, he cried:

' "The hungry sheep look up and are not fed!" You see! That's it, don't you get it?'

And vanished, to a volley of coughs and a powerful explosion coming from under the table, from Mrs Plenty's incredible socialist garters.

'Of course, you're pro-government,' Rose-M had said, once; and when I edgily replied that I most certainly was, and inquired about her own views, she made a pretty face and murmured something about the Liberals. 'I hate tactful answers,' I said, but she laid a hand over my mouth. Then she made a face even prettier, and I forgot about being touchy.

But the feeling that she was a political enemy became very strong after her return from those few days away from home.

Our first meeting had been brief and strangely delightful. Term had begun again at the school of dancing, and Rose-M was dreamily tired when we met and walked through the lanes near her house. I'd come from The Vale, from the nightmarish day's-end rush of people and vehicles; and I told Rose-M how suddenly, above the aching arterial road, there'd appeared an enormous moon. It looked like some serenely considered artistic construct – an object created purely to give quite exotic pleasure; and I'd been greatly consoled by it. As we walked, it floated above us, not so huge as earlier but still . . . curiously insistent on being circular . . . indeed a perfect project for a moon. 'An ideal moon and an ideal Rose-M', I murmured, very happy. I said I was glad not to have to choose which of them I'd prefer to see in the sky. Much as I delighted in having her as an earthly companion, it would be pleasant to look up and to be able to say: 'That's my Rose-M up there! She's full tonight, dear lass!'

Rose-M said she didn't know how she'd get on without my nonsense. I enumerated various features of hers without which I'd feel similarly lost. She said:

'Oh, when are you going to sleep with me?'

'Ha!' I said; in this trance-like happiness not even surprised. 'Ha!' I said again, like one responding to some unurgent philosophical question, and made an enigmatic face; as if indeed she might, in reference to this inquiry, care to consult my thesis when it came out in three or four years time . . .

'Oh,' she said, and leaned close to me, and we staggered drunkenly forward under the moon; and nothing mattered but that quivering closeness.

I went home and worked out a sensible scheme for our union and the prosecution of our careers. Inwardly I was beaming, and continued to wear this pleased expression until we met again, the following evening. At the sight of her, an instant sensation of foolishness possessed me. I felt gauche, even positively coarse. She had to leave me early, she said, because friends were coming to dinner. I was overwhelmed by the distance between my social world and one in which people dined at other people's houses.

A chill of exclusion settled on me.

Wouldn't I come and have lunch with her and her father in London, at the weekend? He was having a very busy time, and was on the brink of a long foreign tour. We must meet . . . I mumbled evasively. The idea filled me with acute terror. How could I do that? I should make a nervous fool of myself. I imagined myself, tongue-tied, felling furniture, in my marmalade suit.

I had a cough, which knocked me about as if I were doing badly in a boxing ring. Rose-M said I ought to wear a scarf. Now unable to be anything but clumsy, I said she was fussier than my mother. Rose-M said quietly that she was sorry about that. She looked at her watch and said she must fly. When she'd gone I wondered if she'd held her face up for a kiss and, in my general seizure of clumsiness, I'd not understood it. I ran raging home. The affair must come to an end! There was nothing but hell and heartache ahead! How long would she put up with my gaucherie? As for my simple homely plan for our future – oh God!

I thought bitterly of our meetings, since that one in which our hands had first flown together. It had been a sequence to make one weep! Beginning complacently marital, I'd swept on to despair, to a dreamlike happiness, and to my present cringing misery. It was like being in a swing at the fair – now monstrously up, now awfully down.

We were to meet the following afternoon, in London. 'Outside the National Gallery?' Rose-M had proposed. Once, when I'd spoken of a visit there, she'd said: 'I always mean to go, but don't. You'll take me, won't you?' I felt, now, like some cultural bully. If we entered the place, it would be much as if I'd frogmarched her into it. Those handsome aviators with whom she'd spent the war – they'd hardly be so gauche as to drag a pretty girl into the National Gallery . . .

When I woke next morning I felt like someone who was, within hours, to be executed several times over. It was one of the worst days of my week at The Vale. I should, among other fatal appointments, be facing the brisk firing squad of my arithmetic division in the staffroom. When they'd finished me off, I should drag myself along to another death in Rose-M's presence – slow throttling by my own gaucherie, most likely.

Surely I *must* disentangle myself from her! Yes, that I *must* do! Regarded rationally, there was nothing to terrify in the fact of someone . . . oh, having lived abroad, as on several occasions she had done. There was no cause for any of these perfectly grotesque miseries of mine. Yet I was not rational. Simply, I was terrified by the whole style of Rose-M's life.

She was outside my world in her delicacy, her swiftness! There was a little notebook of hers I'd seen once, prettily bound, with a rosemary flower embossed in one corner, and the word '*Pensées*'.

Fool! What did her having a pretty notebook have to do with my ability to behave well to her or otherwise?

Perhaps I should not even go to meet her?

And then the day at The Vale was curiously bearable. I even discovered that, unexpectedly, I'd convinced Lightfoot ii of the utility of decimals. I'd noticed him the day before staring at the county cricket averages printed in a handbook. 'Of course,' I said, 'those are decimals.' I felt an unctuous sort of triumph, and expected Lightfoot to sneer at me. I should certainly deserve that. Instead, his jaw dropped, and he asked: 'How can they be?' I gave a simple demonstration. Lightfoot was amazed by this marriage of what he most loved with his profoundest detestation. 'Divide the number of runs by the number of completed innings,' he informed himself, over and over again.

'You could work out your average for last season,' I said. I thought his heart might stop. 'And Hazard's?' 'Oh yes. And Hazard's!'

This morning I discovered that, having worked on his own record and those of his friends – and enemies – Lightfoot was busy checking the averages given in the handbook. Before the lesson was over he was pressing these well beyond the conventional two figures after the decimal point. 'Denis Compton's average,' he called me over to be informed. '63·592871562938421072 . . . and I haven't finished!'

So I felt unnaturally buoyant as I went to meet Rose-M. Oh yes, the process of disentanglement should begin, and I was sure I could do it perfectly coolly. All the fever had been my own creation. The affair would prove capable of being politely, even casually dissolved. I would simply go scuttling down the ladder again, away from all that monstrous strain and unbearable glory!

I'd never been so struck by the special quality of her face – its narrow colourfulness, the bright sensitiveness of her expressions. She was wearing red slacks, a pale coat informally tied. I took her hand with enormous pride, and attempted absurdly to retain it as we passed through the National Gallery's turnstiles.

Then we were lost among pictures . . .

We were staring at Rubens' *Rape of the Sabines*. What very large women! I thought. And how close the blood was to the skin! They seemed boiled, rather! Or as if they had been drinking far too much, and the flush had come out all over! They were trying hard to seem terrified, yet their general appearance of repletion was somehow hostile to any notion of terror.

'Oh dear,' said Rose-M.

'What *nice* ladies!'

'Do you like us like that? With everything . . . *swelling out*?'

'I was thinking,' I said, 'that ladies so massive might be *harmless*.'

'Oh, of course,' said Rose-M, and fell into happily displeased silence.

In front of the Arnolfinis she said: 'I'd look very queer, do you know? – *pregnant*.' And then: 'Will you mind?'

I led her to the Rokeby Venus, which had become part of my sensual furniture when I was in my teens. I'd prepared Rose-M to be impressed. The lady lay on that swelling haunch and gave her unurgent attention to the unlikely fragment of face in the mirror. 'Your trouble,' said Rose-M, 'is that you've fallen in love with women who are nothing but paint.'

'Rather unusual paint,' I said.

'Pshaw,' said Rose-M. 'What you need is women of flesh and blood.' She glared at the Rokeby Venus over imaginary pince-nez. 'I mean, just one real woman.'

We walked across Trafalgar Square, under the Admiralty Arch, into the Mall. A full moon was scrawled over by the bare branches of trees.

'A huge dilapidation of palaces,' I said.

We kissed and murmured, and time ran loose.

'Do you really like me?' I asked.

'What a silly question to put to someone who's just been kissing you.'

'I didn't know whether kissing meant liking.'

'Oh, that makes me out to be a horrible type of person.'

'You see—I think so often: how could Rose-M really like me?'

She interrupted my words with small kisses.

'And I wonder,' I said, 'whether the things that matter to one of us really matter to the other.'

'Yes, I know. I wonder about that too. So many things matter to you—so few things matter to me . . . But oh—you've said you love me. How could you say that and . . . be so unsure?'

'Tonight I'm sure—I'm sure!'

'You see, I know I could make you *very* happy. I'm certain of that.'

'Rose-M—'

'You make me laugh, and I make you laugh . . . sometimes.'

The war seemed curiously to linger along this great faded vista. About the monumental buildings there was an air of more than wintry dilapidation. I felt, in a strange form – melancholy and happy at once – the sensation I'd had ever since I was a little boy, coming into London: the awe, was it? – the slightly unsteady astonishment felt by the suburbanite in the capital . . . As if his behaviour ought to be much larger and bolder than usual.

I'd never felt such a combination of comfort and excitement. We were settled into the warmest of present moments – our bodies moved slowly along the Mall like a single creature – and yet expectation was there, was crouching, was promising that there should be . . . such a springing, soon, into the future . . .

Oh now, surely, I should cease to be a fool! From now on, my crazy diffidence would no longer prevent me from harvesting what appeared to be so freely, so sweetly proffered?

3

Suddenly there was talk of examinations. 'Let's see,' said Mr Diamond. 'Upper Five History—safe in your hands, eh?'

We'd hardly, that I could recall, done more than cock an occasional ear over the wall of the monastery, picking up a distracted hint or two of the general situation in the medieval world beyond. It seemed monstrous to think of examining the results of my roaring encounters with Upper Five. In other fields, I attempted to add together the things I'd taught. There seemed nothing substantial enough in any direction to justify more than, say, five minutes of relaxed oral questioning. The formality of an examination paper was quite unsuitable, in all cases.

'Send your papers to Miss Cross to be duplicated,' I was told.

Oh Lord! That meant I would be exposing to the entire world of The Vale the probably asinine questions that, when it came to it, I should bring myself to concoct! How dreadful! I had long been in the habit of rubbing my blackboard clean at the end of each lesson, to keep my work on it a secret from the world. But examinations threatened to make everything public.

I woke up one night from a dream of my expulsion from The Vale. Surrounded by cubs and scouts, I stood in the centre of the playground, being sartorially disgraced in the manner of Dreyfus – Mr Juniper was wrenching off the lapels of my marmalade suit, and I knew that he would next attack the flaps on the pockets. Rose-M stood close at hand, alluringly masquerading as a cub. Mr Beesley came bounding among us, his head a wolf's. 'Would it distress you,' he was asking, with his usual mildness, 'if, um, I made a meal of you?' Mr Juniper said: 'It is the only possible fate for one who has most dreadfully stained the reputation of a very important school.'

I'd been among Old Wolves lately, at a cubbing conference to which Miss Frome had dispatched me. I thought I had never seen men and women so unvulpine. One man, in a queue for tea and biscuits, had addressed me fervently. 'The best years of one's life, would you not say, are spent among the boys?' Then he'd dug into his pocket and brought out a pair of spectacles, through which he'd examined me. 'My word, you're hardly more than a boy yourself.'

Well, I was coming up to twenty-seven, I thought, and ageing fast. I began now to believe that I'd truly been set free from the land, from the agricultural work to which I'd been chained for nearly six years. It was astounding, the effect of the release from war, from that prison where things had stood still, so that one had not been conscious of growing at all. Now, I felt, I was undergoing belated maturation, rapidly – in all fields but those, dammit, of love, and of being at ease in the world.

Why was I so apologetic about being alive? Why could I not be disagreeably assertive? It was being at the hinge of one of the famous British processes of social mobility, I supposed. My father's generation of our family had been the first leaf of the hinge – the clerkly sons of stonemasons, van drivers. In my generation, the grammar school experience had ensured that we formed the other leaf of the hinge . . . were, like many of my coevals, imitation members of the middle class: were, like a few of us, lost altogether in the cracks between the established social roles.

The Vale and Rose-M together were making me exhaustingly aware of the price one might pay for failing to belong, socially. Reason and philosophy could not prevent the retreats and recoilings, the self-accusations and self-blamings, that consumed so much of my spirit.

Mr Raisin smiled at me over some shared allusion to his favourite poet, and I wondered if he would believe how I flopped into each week at The Vale, like a spiritless swimmer into very cold sea, and splashed my way awkwardly from weekend to weekend.

I marked my exam papers furtively, struggling with feelings of pure terror. Were these perhaps the worst exam papers ever completed in a school of the calibre of The Vale? I saw the expensive hopes of parent after parent being shattered by the incredibly inaccurate view of the medieval monastery expressed by Upper Five (could anyone hope to enter, say, Charterhouse on the strength of such assertions as that 'they dinned in the refuctory'?); the pure anti-arithmetic of my backward set: the amazing stance in respect of simple parsing of my Middle Three: and Upper Three's cheerful willingness to regard the parts of speech as a sort of . . . general jam. The last was to me the most macabre: even clever children like Jonathan Honey seemed, under my care, to have concluded that a noun might as well be an adjective if caprice didn't cause you to call it a verb.

I wanted to burn all those papers, preferably at midnight, best of all in some remote spot where even the ashes would not betray me. But it was the convention that they should be returned so that boys might note their errors and repair them. I'd have been a shade happier about this if I'd been able to give the instruction: On the appearance of Mr Juniper, without hesitation, swallow your paper . . . But the actual consequence of returning the papers was not one that, even in my madly sensitive anticipation of disaster, I had foreseen. Scores of boys were ready to dispute my marking. They questioned the marks given for each section of a paper: they demanded a recount of the total number of marks. At The Vale, I was to learn, boys took their revenge for the general terror of being examined by being extremely nasty about the results. I fought action after action, like some lawyer crazily over-employed. Till the very end of term I was beating off subtle attempts to have a mark added here or there, some readjustment made to a form order. Many boys kept files of their marks, as they accumulated, and of the points of complaint they were pursuing. It wasn't revenge only, I thought: it was also an example of the intense competitiveness of private education. You could expect to rise or fall, to realize your parents' ambition for you or to fail to do so, by the loss or gain of a mark.

In the end, I was not ungrateful for all this. It meant that boys felt some motive for being at school after the examinations were over. I trembled to think what a completely motiveless class might have done with me.

On the last day of term, snow fell. It was, as it turned out, the first act in one of the most fearful of our winters. There'd been bad patches earlier: fog making the world a place of imprisonment, down whose wretched walls ran streams of icy water. But there'd been pleasant days in between. And now in the streets there was this thick white silence, very beautiful. I walked out of school and there, waiting, was the dark-faced boy in Lower Six who had remained my most devoted enemy.

No one liked him. Something drove him to constant malice and distemper. It was like having a bad-natured dog at one's heels. A week or so before, I'd addressed at him one of those speeches of mine that amazed me as I uttered them: they sounded so much like translations from the antique Latin. 'In and out of school, anywhere at all, I've met no one so insolent as you are!' Such speeches seemed to bristle with specially chosen syntactical difficulties. I had no idea where they came from: but clearly there was some tie-up deep within me between indignation and complex formal grammar. Then I'd given the boy a detention.

In the street that last day he crushed snow together in his hands and said: 'Now you're going to get something for all the rotten things you've done this term!'

Oh really, it wouldn't do! I gave way to none in the relentless displeasure with which I assessed my term's work. I hadn't yet taught a decent lesson. Indeed, one lesson followed another without design, often in the face of all logic. I'd tacked, in a panic-stricken fashion, back and miserably forth, in my attempts to understand the weather of my pupils' moods.

I'd been a hopeless disciplinarian – whatever that was. Lightfoot ii, now tender towards me as the man who had demonstrated a link between maths and cricket, said: 'You always tell Hazard and Dennis to see you afterwards – but you always go away before they can!' It was true. Once a lesson was over, I wanted nothing so much as to hide in the staffroom. I didn't want to stay and follow up half-forgotten petulances.

I was ashamed of myself, for the cowardly paradox that lay between my deep dislike for teaching, and my inability to confess as much to people who seemed to trust and think well of me. I smiled valiantly, but all within was plaintive defeat.

Yes: all these terrible things were true. But I wasn't going to accept

86

my dark-faced enemy's judgment. A melancholy view of life was one thing: a sour and melodramatic one, quite another. I muttered 'Idiot!' and went crunching through the fresh snow. My back winced from snowballs as yet unlaunched.

The need to write reports had come as a final assault on my battered conscience. It seemed to me that I should be writing: 'I have taught this boy badly and offer, for the little they are worth, my apologies': or simply, 'I could have done better.' Instead I was required to add cowardly libel to my crimes. It might be true that Nye, in my arithmetic set, had made very little effort: but ought I not, in all decency, to add that he'd found himself in the hands of a teacher peculiarly unable to command effort?

Worse – I'd discovered that the common quality of most report-making at The Vale was one of wit, edge, a pleasant slyness. Of one boy, Mr Hollow had scrawled in a handwriting that seemed curiously to reflect the slurred character of his speech: 'Often absent: and when present, still absent.' 'James,' someone had written, 'seems indignant because Latin is not English. Once he withdraws this objection, all should be well.' I didn't know what contribution I could make at this level. And the things I wanted to say about boys were too complex to be rendered down to the phrases – conventional or not – of a school report. What, for example, could I say of little Tudor? He'd made an important contribution to the end-of-term concert, playing his cello most beautifully. The instrument had almost blotted him out. There'd been this large brown cello, with Tudor's nervous hands requiring music from it. Afterwards, he'd skipped up to me and said: 'So you see, sir – I *can* play!'

It amazed me that this small gifted boy had believed that I'd had doubts about his talent. But then I'd exhibited very plain doubt of his power over formal English grammar. He'd danced up to me once in class – he seemed to think that approaching a master in a sort of demented jig would help to make the event imperceptible – and asked me if he was doing the right exercise. My eye had fallen on numerous very false assertions about various categories of noun. 'These are . . . not quite correct,' I'd murmured. Oh! how could such tenderly indefinite reproaches ever bring about an improvement in his work? These statements of his were monstrously off the point, and I should say so in round schoolteacherly terms. 'You haven't quite got it, I think!' His jig became really frenetic. 'Oh no, sir! Oh please, no sir! I didn't want you to say anything about my work. I only wanted to know if I was doing the right exercise.' 'And perhaps' – I obliged myself to be sterner – 'there should be fewer blots.' 'Oh sir, stop it! Just tell me if I'm doing the right exercise. Then I'll go back and get on!' Which he did, now performing a fair tarantella: longing, one saw, to whirl himself into invisibility.

I found myself, at heart, very much in Tudor's state. The savage academic demands of Common Entrance appalled me as they did him. All those exercises, in this subject and that, the ferocities of grammar English, French and Latin: the massive mysteries of geometry, the schoolman's algebra ... At heart I had the morale, not of a teacher, but of a dunce. Heaps of exercise books filled me with much the same oppression and dismay as I'd have felt if I'd watched servants of the Inquisition hurrying about with the paraphernalia of torture and execution. I understood so well little Tudor's feeling that he was being inscrutably tested, and largely with reference to crises of knowledge and understanding of which, left to himself, he could easily have remained intelligently unaware. 'Music,' said Mr Beesley, having Tudor in mind, 'is a kind of clever stupidity, I suppose.' He was rash enough to say this in the hearing of Mrs Dorset, the part-time music mistress, who gave him a brief, packed lecture on the mental majesty of, in the main, Bach and Mozart. Fond though I was of Mr Beesley, I enjoyed that. One at least of the staffroom's negligent aphorisms had been struck to the ground, and there beaten to dust by passionate conviction.

Beyond even Mrs Dorset's vehemence was the school secretary's view of music as one of the more blatant absurdities of the curriculum. Miss Cross had spoken severely of another performer at that end-of-term concert, a pianist. 'I heard him practising,' she told us. 'It took him *so long* to get from one note to the next! I said: "Come on! It's just – *straight ahead! Straight ahead, and carry on and get it over with!* That's the way to play music!"'

But I enjoyed, I really did enjoy, that concert, as I was to feel ridiculous delight in so much end-of-termishness. Such occasions seemed to be festivals of forgiveness and forgetfulness as to the agonies and horrors of term. Mr Diamond became almost ungovernably affable. He had, one knew, as little patience with the more delicate aspects of music-making as Miss Cross. 'I like,' he'd once confessed, 'a good brass band, or a good bellow. Oh, I know it's an old-fashioned point of view. But there it is. I like a bit of *blood* in things! A bit of *go*! I'm not too fond of these concerts where you have to *strain* to hear what's going on.' Harrod Parker and I imagined, somehow, Mr Diamond as a music-goer throughout the years at the Albert Hall and elsewhere, always bending forward, ear always cupped: hopeful but, as the years passed, less and less patient as to the endless finicky pianissimo of classical music ...

The Vale was short of brass bands and Mrs Dorset had never seen fit to give such instruction as would lead to good bellows. But in the high-spiritedness of term-end Mr Diamond allowed his admiration to cover such things as madrigals, faint solos on the recorder, hesitant subtleties on the piano. 'Oh, very good, lad!' His mellow approval, expressed also with those immense hands of his, came like thunder on the tail of every instrumental and vocal tenderness. 'Oh, my goodness, that was *well tried*!'

Mr Juniper had displayed his own, but more candid and impatient, delight in the concert, the final Running-over, house parties, and similar events: all of which seemed to turn The Vale for some days into a kind of panting indoor circus. I'd grown very fond of Mr Juniper – or perhaps I should say that I'd come to enjoy the legendary figure he'd been turned into: partly, I imagine, by accident, partly by such an accretion of mannerisms (and anecdotes relating to them) as might attach itself to any lively schoolmaster after forty years: but partly by his own manipulation. Mr Juniper enjoyed, one could see, being half-fictitious. He cultivated, among other things, a way of suddenly diving into a scene, and bringing it to a halt by some totally unlikely inquiry. So he'd enter a class and pose a grammatical puzzle. Important expositions might be ruined by such intrusions: a silence carefully secured might be smashed beyond repair. He was a cause, always, of excitement. Mr Juniper was no grey figure, no invisible presence. He brought to any situation the preoccupations and problems that happened to be in his head at the time. So, on occasions, that startling entry of his into a classroom might herald some apparently quite inappropriate request for information. 'Who on earth won the county cricket championship in 1919?' It was often about cricket that he made these appeals or set his posers. Lightfoot ii, monstrously ill-behaved and successfully idle, could do little wrong in Mr Juniper's eye, being rarely found wanting as an authority on cricket. And Lightfoot, many had noticed, was more often than not one of those who were named for second helpings at school lunch. Mr Juniper, charmingly unscrupulous in his use of patronage, held firmly in his grasp the right to name those who should finish up The Vale's splendid dishes. In another setting one might have thought it quite unhealthy, the excitement – as of a gaming room – that was generated as to second helpings. Mr Juniper, handsome, sparkling, would stand at the serving table, a ladle in hand, and would begin formally enough with any boy whose birthday fell on that day. The price to be paid – by him and the others who, for this subtle reason or that, were hailed to the serving table – was the character sketch and current report with which Mr Juniper would accompany such an award. 'Liss major is twelve today, so he says, though some of us doubt that. Liss major's father was out for a duck in both innings in the Winchester-Harrow match of 1925. Liss has a very pretty sister who seems to have attracted the attention of a classmate of his who should be giving his mind to geometry and Latin. Eh, Pargeter? It's no good holding that plate out any longer, Liss. How is your mother, by the way? Off you go, now! Lightfoot minor!' And Liss, grinning complicatedly, half-appalled and half-delighted by this set of breathless slanders, would bear off his reward, a fragment perhaps of a splendid pudding I have met nowhere but at The Vale, a lightness of sponge infused with an impression as of a half a dozen rare and superbly nameless jams.

Passing behind me on his way to his seat at the end-of-term concert, Mr Juniper quickly reset my shoulders and murmured a charmingly hostile comment on my tie. I felt that the disasters of the past weeks were finally muffled. I was, for this absurd moment, a successful and accepted young usher on the brilliant staff of this important school. I was an officer in the camp of my social enemies. I allowed myself to feel modestly swollen-headed.

And then Miss Frome told me that Miss Seakins had told her that she'd overheard Mr Hollow saying I was a useful man. I felt then as though I'd accomplished my life's mission and could quite cheerfully bring it to an end. 'HERE LIES EDWARD BLISHEN', my tombstone would state, ungloomily. 'A USEFUL MAN. CONTENTEDLY WITHDREW FROM LIFE, December 19, 1946'.

Odd, odd! that this school term, to me so painful and disastrous, should outwardly wear so many signs of moderate success!

I was not, then, in any mood to submit to my dark-faced enemy, out there in that first snow of the winter. He stalked me all the way to my bus. I was, I thought, as simple a target as anyone could wish for: yet not one of his snowballs, thrown at however short a range, struck me in a spot that was really uncomfortable. I was the least ruffled of Saint Sebastians, striding with careful insouciance towards the Christmas holidays, the dilemma posed by Rose-M (or by myself in respect of Rose-M) – and, inevitably, though I'd rather not think of that, towards the raw realities of my second term.

That night I found my School Certificate, but realized that to pursue my inquiries about matriculation, I'd need also my birth certificate. This was not to be found.

But things had happened, no doubt of it, that might be bundled together hopefully under some such phrase as . . . fair progress. Could do far better, but might have done even worse.

'LOVE', my intimate report might have read. 'Shows no grasp of this subject at all. After a promising start, a very disappointing slide into apathy and stupidity. (Signed) R. Perkins.'

Rose-M was going to yet another farm, this time in Northumberland, for Christmas. She seemed to have spent the war making friends with Wing Commanders and lofty office-holders in the WAAF, who had returned from battle to resume their lives on estates, invariably large, in parts of the country always far from London. 'You could come with me,' Rose-M had said. 'Oh, you could so easily come with me, you know. Any friend of mine is a friend of theirs. Oh Edward, it would be fun!' Then she'd contemplated my hopelessly miserable expression. 'Oh, I wish you were more . . . ordinary! You know, there are men who'd . . . well, they'd not be backward in accepting such an invitation. To be frank, I'd have a job to keep them away! Oh!'

How could I go home, I wondered, and inform my parents that I was spending Christmas in Northumberland with a girl whose name I'd not previously mentioned to them? I kept Rose-M a complete secret from my family. They would, in a simple, earnest, hopeful way, treat her as . . . oh, what were the terms? as my *intended*, my *young lady*. The experimental ambiguity of our relationship – and merely Rose-M's habit of moving about the country, from the home of one friend to another – would cruelly mystify them. They'd hardly accept that I could do anything so grave as to spend Christmas among strangers at the behest of a young woman without being within an ace of marriage. They would make kindly, impossible jokes, and litter my way with tender hints and innuendoes.

But I'd never get so far as that – clearly I had no hope of reaching that advanced stage of confession and candour. I was too bashful to mention Rose-M's existence to them. They'd heard rumours, they'd made something of a remark of James's, the comment of a neighbour. There was a girl, they believed. But they came no nearer than this – and oh, it was too near, even this for me was too awfully near!

Rose-M said: 'But you must at least meet my father. Why do you never agree to come when he's there?'

I escaped from all such questions, when I could, by simple retreat into the rich happiness offered by her bosom and other reposeful parts. There'd been one or two evenings when, indifferent to weather, we'd trodden a tangled, moony path among the lanes around Rose-M's house. Then a union of fingers, a sudden urgent jamming together of our bodies as if, from one second to the next, they'd been turned into magnets: some playing with hair, or dreamy gazings and leanings together, would drive away all awkward discussion. We'd talk contented nonsense. The world seemed complete, on these occasions, needing no support of everyday activity – a perfect universe of murmurings and wanderings and caressings. Families? announcements? contracts and arrangements? Being approved by relations and friends? Saving money, and spending it? What had such things to offer relevant to the total delight of those hours in the December darkness, under the spanking bareness of trees in the winds of that winter that had yet to hint at the brutal coldness it had in store?

When I emerged from these trances – when, that is, the world of everyday affairs reasserted itself – my despair was always great. Of course Rose-M could not be content with these unlocated paradises, disjoined from families, friends, from all the social bustle that she enjoyed. 'There are so many people I'd love you to meet – and I'd love them to meet you,' she'd sigh, as we walked into or out of these paradises. Or: 'I'm trying to imagine you in the *George and Dragon*. Oh, you'd really look rather well in the *George and Dragon*, Edward! You really would!'

And just before the end of term at The Vale, and when I'd made my wretched face after she'd repeated the invitation to Northumberland, Rose-M said, with a quite fierce firmness: 'Now, I've got news for you! On Thursday evening you're coming to see us, socially. Daddy's away in Denmark, but mummy will be there, and my sister whom you haven't *really* met, and her young man, who you'll think is rather dull, but he's sweet really only rather silent, I have to admit – anyway, you're coming, at eight o'clock exactly; and I warn you, my dear man, that if you let me down I shall hold no further intercourse with you. And that reminds me of something I'd like to suggest but you'd think it appallingly coarse, so I'll leave it for the moment and simply repeat: Thursday evening, eight o'clock sharp, at "Grantham", Coppice Road. And don't look so miserable, because for once it's not going to help you.' And she'd given me a positively militant kiss and then flounced off, into a darkness that seemed to me fairly impenetrable and possibly not of this world at all.

4

'Play!' cried Rose-M. 'Play! Please *do* play!'

I'd never been so close to such an enormous piano. The keyboard smiled into the highly polished woodwork, and the reflection of its large even teeth reached me where I sat hunched and unwillingly grumpy on the sofa.

'He plays?' said Mrs Perkins. 'Oh, how wonderful! You *must* play for us, Edward! Oh, *do* give us that pleasure! Chopin, please!' She turned to Rose-M. 'With Edward it *would* be Chopin, don't you think?'

Rose-M gave me her divided look: the happily embarrassed half-smile that meant she knew how I'd hate this, but agreed with her mother. 'You don't like mummy,' said the look, 'but you like me and I am very like her.' Her smile seemed to enjoy this fiendish paradox.

'I really don't play,' I said. 'I make a noise for myself. Privately, I do that. I mean, I never do play when there are other people.'

To my relief Mrs Perkins was content to incorporate this into the careless legend, half-whimsical and half-malicious, that she was weaving round me. 'Of course, Edward *would* be shy,' she told Rose-M. I guessed she knew very well that it hurt people to be turned into whimsical characters. I grew grumpier still.

On my arrival in the house my body had lost all coherence and my mind had fallen apart. My formal entry and welcome were delayed. I'd stood in my ruined state in the hallway, listening to a voice from upstairs, and bouncing sounds. These came from Rose-M's elder sister, Jenny. She was uttering cries that I pieced together as meaning that everything had been lost, stolen, or had not been replenished. Theft and domestic negligence had left her wardrobe empty. 'Oh, *Rose-M* . . . where is my new head-scarf?' 'Oh, *mummy*, my little brooch . . .' Rose-M and Mrs Perkins were standing in the hall, rebutting these charges. I half-thought that Jenny might come bounding down the stairs naked. In fact when at last she appeared she was spectacularly over-dressed. Rose-M and her mother set about her at once, relieving her of items of clothing and jewellery that they claimed were not hers. 'Oh darling, have we got to go into that again? Daddy gave it to *me*!' Somehow in the midst of all this I was introduced; somehow, Jenny distinguished the reference from all those others to disputed pieces of property. She gave me a smile subliminal in its brevity. 'Jenny's very nice really!' Rose-M murmured. 'Well, I'm off,' Jenny said, 'and we must do some *talking* about *things* in the morning.' She flashed a smile at me, inconsequently radiant, and then went quite blank, as if her face had been electrically overloaded, and had fused. Then she said: 'Come on, Peter.' Whereupon from the shadowy neighbourhood of a large hat-stand stepped a young man. I'd not noticed him before. His face looked as though it had been diluted. It had the appearance of a face that was not up to standard, somehow. He nodded frugally and accompanied Jenny up the garden path towards a racy-looking motorcar that stood outside the gate.

'Forgive us,' said Mrs Perkins. 'A houseful of girls is a madhouse, as you see. My daughters say I'm the worst, and I expect that's so. I have never quite grown up.'

'My goodness,' I said: aware too late of the tone of thick horror with which I spoke.

'Mummy's skittish,' said Rose-M. I found myself confusedly taking this for a statement about Mrs Perkins' nationality, and became deeply panic-stricken. I was set, I knew, on a course where all my reactions would be out of place. Now, for example, I was saying: 'Oh, *really*?' The intonation was that of interest passionately aroused. I appeared to be asking for a long development of Rose-M's remark . . . But she was guiding me into the living room. The doorway seemed criminally narrow, and I managed to hit the frame as I entered with a force great enough to send me spinning obliquely into the room. 'He wants,' Rose-M chose to inform her mother, 'to write.' 'Not really,' I muttered, under the appalled impression that she was urging Mrs Perkins to provide me with instant pen and paper. I fell on the sofa as into a safety-net, bringing my elbow down on the louder end of the piano as I did so. Then, moved by the idea that men should not be seated before women, I leapt to my feet again. It struck me I might now seem to be waiting impatiently for the arrival of stationery, so I sat, striking the keyboard once more. 'So you write poetry?' Mrs Perkins asked, as though this followed from my accidents with the piano, or from my jack-in-the-box treatment of her sofa. I cackled then on a very high note, to show that I was quite at ease, and said, 'Oh no. That is, yes. Sometimes.' Mrs Perkins said: 'Well, I wish you would get Rose-M to do a little writing. She's quite illiterate.'

Of course, that was true, I thought. It was also true, as I'd recently discovered, that she liked windows with diamond panes: which, for some reason, filled me with a sort of ideological rage. Then Mrs Perkins began her teasing: torture, one might call it, by the invention of whimsical characteristics for a guest. I was clearly only one in a succession of young fools who had been through this process – Rose-M's followers. All had sat on this sofa. None, I guessed, had treated it as I had done, or in sinking into it had struck that really quite distant piano with their elbows: or had been in such danger of grotesquely misunderstanding every remark addressed at them. Inside my flustered frame sat my self, my spirit, whatever it was – a pilot finding himself once more aloft in an aircraft quite pitifully ramshackle. My self abandoned the useless controls: folded his arms and sighed, gravely.

I was certain that, behind her most elaborate spectacles, Mrs Perkins – from time to time – was winking at me. 'You realize, I suppose,' would be the meaning of the wink, 'that Rose-M has a stream of lovers (timetabling their visits is no easy task), and all the others adore dancing and pubs and . . . windows with little diamond panes?'

I was numb with misery . . . yet my moral circulation was constantly being part-restored by nods and smiles from Rose-M. Now and then she provided her mother with material for her teasings – 'You really should see Edward with his crocodile going to the football ground!' – but at the same time, especially with the sweetness and secrecy of her smile, she seemed to understand my despair, and to wish to be associated with it. She moved round the room, delicate and bright, and I felt like a compass in some magnetically incoherent setting: my spirit soaring, as I reacted to Rose-M, and slumping awfully, as I was drawn again by the shine of Mrs Perkins' spectacles, wrought of some unfamiliar substance and amazingly shaped so that they seemed not so much an aid to vision as a work of art propped on an unusual easel.

The evening passed . . . Mrs Perkins went to bed ('Don't keep Edward up too *painfully* long!' she advised Rose-M, but I guessed that she put it that way round out of her rather spiky politeness) . . . And then we were in a different world altogether. Within minutes, the first part of the evening had dropped into a preposterous limbo.

'Oh,' said Rose-M as I took up a position of dizzy vantage, as close as possible to her various brightnesses. 'Oh my goodness. All *that*!'

I took it that she was referring to the entirely irrelevant events of the evening. The only relevance sprang from an intoxication, a faintness that now had me in its grip: had her, too, if I was to judge by her shining eyes, and the long kisses into which she drew me, as if I were being sucked into some fragrant vortex.

'Oh,' I said. 'And I didn't see you for weeks.'

'I know. Why? Why?'

'I didn't know if you wanted to see me.'

'Oh – silly!'

'But how awful if you'd said: "I don't want to see you". Or worse – if you'd been polite and said: "Oh, how nice of you . . . ah – come in and have a cup of tea, but I must rush out in a few minutes."'

Were mouths really ever so soft and kindly? Now she coiled in my arms like a kitten. Now she lay face downwards across my breast and I hid myself in her sweetsmelling hair. The confusion of our bodies became extreme. 'I think,' I said, 'this might be my own knee I have my hand on, and am thinking of so tenderly.'

'I try so hard to be honest with you,' she murmured, out of the densest of these tangles, 'and I keep wondering whether I am . . . Oh, you're so good, so sensitive and so easily hurt.'

Again I was not really understanding what was said to me. So I dealt with that doubt of hers, as to her honesty, with such caressings and soothings as might have been appropriate for a cut finger, a wasp sting. Honesty she had (I tasted it on her lips) as she had all other virtues (I applauded these with gentle pressures on her thigh). I brushed aside her description of myself with a drunken chuckle. She need have no fear: I was in fact thoroughly bad, insensitive – perfectly thick-skinned.

'What music do you like?' she was asking. 'I'll tell you what I like, first. I like Frankie Sinatra, and Tchaikovsky, and Rimsky-Korsakov and Dvorak – I like . . . oh, big tunes . . .'

'I like Beethoven – because his music thinks—'

'I knew you would! Oh, that's why I don't like it – I'm too lazy to think . . . Oh, you would grow tired of me so quickly.'

I smiled, as if she'd set out a prospectus for our perfect felicity . . .

And suddenly, I wanted to turn to her for comfort; and, in the melting cave our bodies made, tried to fix on the reason for my need of comfort. It was, I saw at last, a great wish for comfort from Rose-M in respect of all the problems that arose from Rose-M's existence . . .

I'd caught sight of an object in the turnings of our limbs, and had decided it was my watch, and had read the time – half-past two – when there came the sound of a car drawing up outside the house.

'Jenny and Peter,' murmured Rose-M: but then there was a knock on the window, a rap of knuckles. 'Oh,' she cried. She flew for her comb: flew back for the brooch that held her blouse together. 'Tidy your hair,' she whispered urgently, and was gone.

From the hall came the sound of a deep voice, jocular: with Rose-M's, high, surprised, delighted. I sprawled, stupefied, where so recently there'd been our murmuring warmth. The door opened and in came a tall man, tweedy.

'Do you know Edward? An old – ah . . . We belong to the same – discussion group. Edward – Tom Randall.'

My hand was seized and wrung with an enthusiasm that seemed at once whole-hearted and meaningless. 'At school together,' he said.

Of course. He'd been a paying pupil and rugby footballer. Very sporting, altogether. There'd been the barrier between us that existed between scholarship boys and paying pupils: between the school's sportsmen and its . . . loungers, as the headmaster had called us. Not active dislike – a sort of apathy. In any case, our social worlds had been very different. Tom Randall had always lived at the leafy end of the town.

He was gazing at Rose-M, gluttonously. 'Well, well, little Rose-M,' he was saying. 'My, you *have* grown!' There was in his voice a kind of measuringness: as if he'd actually run Rose-M over with a tape-measure. 'My, yes – you *have*!' he cried. 'Well, well – little Rose-M!' Rose-M said hurriedly, in my direction: 'Tom lives along the road. We haven't met for . . . oh, two or three years, is it?' Randall was still gazing at her computingly: he gave her a vague, warm smile. 'Good Lord,' he said. The simple fact that in three years Rose-M's measurements had not stood still seemed beyond his digestion.

'We've heard a lot of you from your sister,' said Rose-M.

'Well, well,' said Randall. 'And I've heard a lot about you. And been shown photos. You and – mostly RAF types, I think—'

'Oh no – only two, really. I was very consistent,' said Rose-M. I had never before heard her being polite in this fashion. It drained her voice of all expressiveness.

'Well, well,' said Randall, continuing to gaze at her. 'I say, you certainly have grown!'

For the first time in my life I longed for the simple skill of seizing someone by the scruff of the neck and bouncing him about. The vision of doing this to Tom Randall was so sharp that I was surprised to see him still standing there, still frankly agape at the growth of Rose-M's chest.

'Been home for a whole week,' he was saying. 'But, my dear,

haven't run into you. Not in the *Red Lion*. Not in the *Albion*. Where do you hang out now? Who's your crowd?'

'I'm at the Academy,' said Rose-M. 'Doing dance. So in London more than here.'

'I—' Randall broke off. He seemed to be lost in calculations, the thought of which caused me to have fresh visions of violent activity. I had grossly neglected certain studies. '*To frogmarch an impertinent fellow from the room.* Grasp him by the collar and, if possible, also by the seat of the trousers . . .' No, that would be plain ejection. One should—

'Oh good,' he said, and became animated again. 'I tell you what. When you've . . . finished here, come down the road to my place and have a nightcap. I'll run you home,' he added, turning to me.

'Ah yes.' Was there satirical intention in the choice of that word 'finished', or was he incapable of satire? Had my old schoolfellow – ha! – come to certain conclusions about our dishevelment, and the crushed and haphazard lie of the cushions on the sofa? His use of the word had certainly made lingering quite impossible. We couldn't let Randall go and then 'finish' before calling for those unwelcome drinks. 'I think I must be off now, anyway,' I said.

'Oh fine, fine. Oh good. Then you can come straight along with me. That's frightfully good. Come along then.'

While Randall drove his car from her house to his, Rose-M and I walked along the road.

'You don't mind?' she said. 'I don't think I like him, you know. I really haven't had much to do with him.'

'Hmm,' I said, not knowing how to avoid sounding miserable.

'But I wish,' said Rose-M, 'that you . . . liked more people.'

'It's only,' I said hopelessly, 'that he's so . . . hearty.'

'Oh, I *know*!' She seized on the word with a vigour for which I sought an adjective: too quickly discovering it. Her vigour was *hearty*. 'I know. And it's irritating, isn't it? . . .' Then she giggled and gave me a quick sideways look. 'You know what we used to call him, though? *Randy!*'

She giggled again, while immense extra forces of sternness and disapproval formed up inside me as I grasped the implications of this remark. Then Rose-M hurriedly reached up to my chin and brushed it with her lips. 'You don't have to care,' she said.

Randall was waiting for us at the door of his house – his mother's, in fact, Rose-M murmured. Glancing through it, I saw a flash of brass: my first impression was that the hall was completely papered with warming pans. There were, in fact, only three of these: but many little shelves and brackets supported other brass objects – kettles, pots, vases: all gleaming. Scores of misshapen images of Rose-M and myself accompanied our entry.

We were led into the living room, and Randall disappeared behind a further door. As he went he called a single word:

'Stout?'

I was again out of touch with meanings. It seemed to me a cry related to the man's amazement about Rose-M's development into a mature woman. Rose-M nudged me. 'Stout, Edward? To drink?' 'Oh, I think so,' I said. She fixed me with her bright eye and sighed. 'Sweetie,' she begged. '*Wake* up!'

It was not a room easy to be awake in. Here the brassiness of the hall was interspersed with a sense of glass and gilt. A great quantity of gewgaws bristled on a wilderness of little shelves. Convex mirrors hung everywhere, reflecting one another. I saw many tiny desirable Rose-Ms attended by an equal number of small despondent versions of myself.

'I say,' said Randall, suddenly in the room again. 'You in business?' This question, accompanied by the thrusting into my hand of a tankard enmeshed in raffia, could hardly have been addressed to Rose-M; yet it was at Rose-M he was looking as he asked it. This fact, added to the sudden peopling of all those mirrors with Randalls, made me terribly confused.

'Ah yes,' I said. 'In fact, *not*. Teaching.'

'Yes,' said Randall. He had handed more raffia to Rose-M: who buried her nose in it. 'You were always pretty brainy.'

'Oh, I don't know.' The idea that one had to be brainy to be a teacher seemed rather strongly entrenched in this quarter of the town. Mrs Perkins had said, about nothing at all: 'We don't have a visit from an intellectual every day of the week' . . . Now I said, 'Very small boys. Very simple teaching.'

'Always *thought* you'd be a dancer,' said Randall. This time he looked at me, and I felt my face burn with astonishment, shame and anger. At once he switched his gaze away and fixed on a nearby mirrored Rose-M. 'You have the shape,' he said.

'It pleased mummy,' said Rose-M. She threw a score of left legs over a score of right legs, while Randall and I gazed together at the performance. 'I think she always wanted to be a dancer's mother.'

'Chaps waiting at the stage door, I suppose,' said Randall.

'Well,' said Rose-M; and I guessed uneasily that, alone with him, she would have dwelt extensively upon this side of things. Now she simply said: 'Well, you know what it's like.'

'Rather.' He turned on her suddenly the full blast of curiously blank eyes. 'Have to be careful,' he said. 'Hard work, I suppose, mostly?'

Rose-M spread herself in her chair, a stretching of arms and legs that filled the walls with tiny fleshcoloured gestures. 'Long for weekends,' she said. 'Doing nothing.'

'I can imagine,' said Randall. He was suddenly very severe. He turned and gave me what, in anyone whose expression could be more certainly related to his emotions, might have been taken for a warning glare. 'You want to be careful, Rose-M,' he said. 'Not overdo it.'

They began talking about their neighbours . . . I was suddenly chilled, in the grip of the sharpest grief and alarm. An hour before, the world had consisted of Rose-M and myself, and our tenderness – groping towards honesty with each other – was in control. Now, suddenly, the world was all these Randalls, these Rose-Ms crossing and uncrossing their legs and talking with a mannered off-handedness: mirrors, brass kettles and waterjugs and crossed hunting horns, a wild multiplication of objects that had been hurled, cruelly, into the happy world of an hour before. It seemed a symbol, a warning. Real though that other world might appear, it could perhaps never resist violation by this Randall world . . .

They were chattering. I felt a dull gratitude for Randall's lack of interest in me. What could I have said about the *Red Lion* set? motor cars? antiques? And such a secret rallying tone in Randall's voice. Calculations and hidden knowledge piled up behind that voice, with its tailings-off, its curious sudden changes of subject. He laughed now and then, about nothing that was being said . . .

At last we could go. 'Dancers need their beauty sleep, I suppose, eh, little Rose-M?' And Rose-M fluttering her eyelids.

'I'll get the car warmed up then and take – ah – Edward home. Shan't be a minute.'

Rose-M transformed again. Her hand fierce in mine. 'Oh, don't look so sad! Please, please . . .'

He was leaning over to open the car door for me. 'Lovely to see you, m'dear.' And again the long measuring stare: the feeling that he was winking to himself, inside. 'See you in the *George*, eh?'

And she had waved her hand and was gone into the shadows across the road.

We drove in silence: then Randall said, abruptly: 'Known Rose-M long?'

'A few months. Oh not longer. Six months or so.' Then I could think of nothing to add. There was nothing whatever, under sun or moon, that I would ever think of to say to Tom Randall.

I made myself ready to stop the car at the top of our road. I didn't want him to watch me enter the semi-detached I lived in: and despised myself for that cowardice.

Randall said: 'Watch her with the baker boy!'

'Oh? Oh, this will do me fine. Drop me here. And thank you.'

'O.K.,' said Randall. Then, when I was half out of the door: 'Remember. Watch out.'

The moon, I noticed as I hurried down the road (as if hoping to carry myself out of reach of that tangle of experiences that I'd spend what remained of the night picking at) – the moon seemed to fall into chimney pots and then be jerked out again by the rise and fall of my tired steps. I felt sick.

It would be bad enough if I knew who he was warning me about. And whether he was warning me on my behalf or his own.

But here I was, hurrying down the road, under the freezing moon: tormented by contrary images of Rose-M. Rose-M loving: Rose-M, chattering. Rose-M with her voice manipulated to impress Tom Randall, even though she had no great liking for him. But such people did not need to be linked by liking. They were united by a whole range of common social experiences and expectations.

She was so lovely! And she had given herself, in those gentle hours, so entirely private to ourselves – she'd given herself to my eyes, my hands, my mouth, with what seemed to me astonishing generosity. Perhaps I was a fool to think so: but I couldn't help believing that such giving must spring, if not from love, then from a trustfulness that came very close to it.

And here I was, now running, and here was our front gate – here I was, in a frozen fatigue, not knowing if I was to watch out for the baker boy or a boy called Baker . . .

Watch out for the baker boy? Watch out for the Baker boy?

Part Three

I

It was a sad Christmas. Rose-M vanished in the direction of that far-off friend. 'Well, you could have arranged something for us, I suppose,' she sighed, before going. 'You really don't seem very good at that, do you?' It was as if the occupant of some tiny unseaworthy vessel, aground a few yards out in the English Channel, had been rebuked for having no firm plans for crossing the Atlantic. The organization of Christmas for two persons was quite beyond my experience. I became, as I was accustomed to be, a hermit: sat indoors and read with gloomy avidity. I also thought over the events of that first term and was amazed and appalled, like someone who realizes belatedly that he's been astray in fog in dangerous mountain country. I'd survived those precipices because I'd not known they were there. How could I go through it all again, in plain daylight?

But there I was, early in that cold January, at the eve-of-term staff meeting. Harrod Parker said it was not at all unnatural to shrink a little from the term to come. But to be filled by it with cringing horror? Well, as to that, he said – he must confess to having suffered once or twice from a nightmare in which he was pegged out on the ground and thousands of ants were crawling over him – all wearing school caps . . .

But oh, I thought, as the staff gathered – what helped, of course, was that things actually happened, and one became absorbed in them. They made it possible to climb out of this deep pit of oneself, full of groaning darkness and misgiving, and to be on the brisk level again, revived by interest in the people who thronged it and the things they did.

There was, for example, a brush between Mrs Leach and Mr Juniper.

Mrs Leach was an exact woman, made rather bitterly so, one felt, by her position as the only full-time lady on the senior staff. I was a little alarmed by her. Approached, she always looked at me with a quivering acidity, as if my being a young male were a bad start. I'd discovered early that one way in which she translated her scorn for young men into action was by pouncing on the least informality of syntax.

'Mrs Leach,' I'd said at one of our first encounters, 'can I come to see you at the end of the morning?'

'I've no doubt whatever that you are perfectly capable of it,' she observed.

I stared at her, puzzled.

'If you *can* you certainly *may*—'

'Oh, I see. I hadn't realized you were being . . . fastidious—'

'Fastidious? Do you think of it in that fashion? I hope you don't persuade Upper Three to share your view. They'll be in trouble from me if so.'

I offered an astonished smile. It became the basic pattern of our exchanges: on her part, dramatically raised eyebrows, a tart twist of the lips: on my part, a smile of astonishment . . .

Mr Juniper's way with her was to feign deafness, or to pass her on to the nearest other person. Both techniques were used at this meeting. He'd read us a letter from a local resident who declared herself under a quite irresistible compulsion to congratulate the school on its public behaviour, making adroit reference as she did so to the school colours and badge. 'It is always a pleasure,' she enthused, 'to catch sight anywhere in the district of Cambridge blue and the sparkling marguerite.'

'Ah, who's that from, sir?' asked Mr Diamond, bluffly.

'A Mrs Manley-Hedges.'

'Ha ha! Very good, sir! . . . Applied recently to have her boy put on the waiting list, I think?'

'The same,' said Mr Juniper. 'Very pleasant woman.'

'Ah yes, sir. Very pleasant woman indeed.'

The shaking of heads down the table amounted to such heavy innuendo – such a verdict on the headmaster's vanity and the use widely made of it by parents of would-be pupils – that I wondered Mr Juniper didn't challenge his staff. But he was enjoying the letter again, reading it to himself and addressing to it the most agreeable nods.

'Really,' Mrs Leach chose that moment to say, 'really, I think the angle at which they wear their caps—'

'Hmm,' said Mr Diamond. He had a trick, at junctures of this kind, of devoting each half of his face to a different opinion. So now, while the profile turned to the headmaster remained bland, that turned to Mrs Leach grunted with agreement.

'So very sloppy . . .' said Mrs Leach.

The headmaster looked up from his letter and frowned. 'What's Mrs Leach saying?' he inquired. He was able at times to give an effect of great pathos to such a query – so that you felt there was something quite callous in taxing the old man's hearing with almost any utterance at all. But Mrs Leach merely raised the pitch of her voice.

'I was saying, Headmaster, that I don't care for the rakish angle at which so many boys are wearing their caps.'

It was not a tactful footnote to Mrs Manley-Hedges' letter. Mr Juniper became highly satirical.

'Oh, are they? I really don't think we can make too much of that. Boys like a little sauciness . . .' Very masculine laughter, all round the table. 'Of course, the *ladies* tend to be jumpy about it. They are at the junior school, certainly.' He leaned away from Mrs Leach and looked enormously disarming, so that there seemed no connection between him and the daggers he was planting in her back. 'I sometimes think our little boys reach the senior school not a moment too soon.'

Mrs Leach leaned away from him in her turn and addressed an amused smile at the end of the room where he wasn't sitting. '*I'm* not jumpy, Headmaster. I can't speak for the junior school ladies, but so far as I am concerned, I cannot allow you to deceive yourself. I am not, myself, at all . . . *jumpy*.' She smiled at the absurdity of this word. 'It is simply a matter of boys being hooligans or not.'

She smiled again: immensely, as though this were a revolutionary new formulation in philosophy.

Mr Juniper bent down to his papers, moving a box file so that it formed a barrier between himself and Mrs Leach. He rustled the papers, allowed one dramatically to catch his attention: then muttered:

'Oh, Mr Diamond – can I ask you to *go into a corner* with Mrs Leach some time and discuss this – ah – detail further?'

One half of Mr Diamond's face beamed his delight. 'Glad to, sir.' The other half somehow divided itself again – expressing, for the benefit of his male colleagues, dismay: and for Mrs Leach, a furious gratification.

This term, as Mr Juniper had promised, I was to be regarded as a member of the senior school staff, with occasional duties in the junior school.

'Damned hard,' said Mr Beesley as we walked to school the first morning, 'coming up from one's junior department to one's senior, under the same management, as it were. No hope of leaving any – um – black marks behind. One's sins cross the road with one!'

'My goodness, yes!' I said – my heart plummeting. Oh God! If this gentle man could make such a reference to my plight, how very severe that plight must be!

The road was full of little boys out of stale nightmares. After all these weeks, did Hazard still exist? Could Dennis be no figment of old fevers, but positive flesh and blood? They greeted me with salutes of an ambiguous kind, but too swift to be analysed for punishable elements.

I rallied, grimly. 'One can hope at best, I suppose, to . . . make people think again about one.' I spared a wretched thought for the thickets of indirectness into which conversation with Mr Beesley always led. Well, this use of 'one,' for instance . . .

'One would attempt that, of course,' said Mr Beesley, trying the pavement ahead of him with the point of his stick. He chuckled sadly and squared his shoulders to take the burden of his thought. 'But one's prospects would hardly exhilarate one! A bad early reputation does so cling, one's noticed!'

One continued one's journey to school in a state of numbness and gloom, murmuring in reply to Mr Beesley's further rounded remarks. And only when one had parted from one's tender tormentor did it occur to one that Mr Beesley had been talking, not of teachers passing from junior to senior school, but of *boys* doing so.

It struck me, once I'd begun the term's teaching, that my lack of faith in myself might now be the chief reason for my distresses. It's true that my struggles with mathematical dunces in the staffroom seemed to have inspired a perverse decision to make me mathematics teacher for the three fourth-year forms – the youngest in the senior school. That reduced considerably my sense of my own credibility. Face to face with the new Lower Four, most of them promoted from the juniors and so familiar, I expected them to demand my credentials. They would swarm round and cry: 'Prove that you know *anything* about decimals, sir!' They would send an instant deputation of protest to Mr Juniper. I was taken aback by their actual innocent acceptance of my role. They listened with unnerving intentness, while I handled elementary arithmetical processes as if they'd been highly controversial novel propositions.

Middle Four – last term's Lower Four – welcomed me with a shameless cheer, which went on for many minutes. Boys leapt on desks and applauded in various ways. I was certain this was out of place. 'Oh that really will do,' I said. A spokesman informed me during a lull that their enthusiasm was genuine. 'We're glad, sir,' he said, horribly amiable.

The new Upper Four – Hazard and Dennis at its heart, though that couldn't be the word – greeted me with its own form of delight. 'Wizard! Smashing!' Hazard shrieked. 'Sorry, sir – oh, *sorry*!' At my entry, Nye fell happily asleep. And a boy called Musk stood up and threaded his way through the uproar to my side. He stroked my hand and said: 'Never mind, sir. They're *beasts*!' Then he added: 'You won't take it hard, will you, if I turn out not to be much good myself? You won't *storm* and *bellow*, will you, like *some masters I can think of*?'

Because of his name, but also because of a decadent quality he had,

Musk was known to the staff as Rosie. He had a round, glowing face, and long eyelashes that he employed as a courtesan might use a fan. He positively *veiled* his eyes. 'At times,' Harrod Parker had said, 'I could swear Rosie was wearing a yashmak.' Yet one might have said that little Musk used his charm and the prettiness of his features in an almost prosaic, practical manner. When his eyelashes swept across his eyes he was also sweeping you out of his way. They were bull-dozers of eyelashes.

'You don't really want me to do a detention, do you, sir?' he might purr in the direction of Harrod Parker – circling round us as we drank our tea at morning break in the hall. 'Sir, you can't want that, can you?'

'Look here, Rosie,' Harrod Parker might say. 'I'd much rather have a good honest kick in the teeth than have you making pretty faces at me like that.'

'But you *don't* want me to do detention, *do* you, sir? Mr Blishen doesn't want you to want me to do detention.' The eyelashes operating in my direction. '*You* don't want Mr Parker to want me to do deten-tion, *do* you sir?'

It worked. Very often it worked. You knew that it was going to work for a whole lifetime. Women would fall for Musk: he was going to cultivate their vulnerability and tendency to enchanted collapse. He would be treacherous, but this would not much alter the case. It was Musk's nature to betray privacies and secrecies, and perhaps he would even be courted for that – for the pleasurable agony of being let down by him. At ten years old he was turning his gifts in that direction on his family. He was always telling us, dropping huge hints, about the quarrelsome relations of his parents. 'Mrs Leach shouts just like my mother when my father has *displeased* her.' Silkily he gave a small stress to the grander words he used. 'Oh don't *hiss*, sir – it reminds me of the sound when my father pours *soda* into his whisky when he's . . . *dissatisfied* with my mother.' He'd clasp his hands behind his back and set his legs apart, sometimes, when he was talking like this: and you could *see* his father . . .

Musk was insistent that I should get married. Against the background of my agonizings over Rose-M, the impatience of this little boy with my bachelorhood struck a bizarre note. Much of the time when I should have been thinking wholeheartedly of decimals, for the benefit of Hazard, Dennis, Musk himself and others, I was . . . oh, hurrying upstairs in some vague thatched cottage far from The Vale in order to clap eyes on our first child. Rose-M was lying there, pale and beauti-ful, and our son was . . . our lovely daughter was . . .

'Sir, you mean *multiply* by 100!'

'That's what I said.'

'No, sir! You said *divide* by 100!' The whole class shrieking me down from that happy bedroom, back to The Vale's attic classrooms . . .

At other times I would be telling myself that if I married Rose-M, it would be like . . . oh, like settling down for the rest of one's life with a stock of novelettes . . .

'You really ought to get married, sir,' Musk would urge. 'You oughtn't to wait much longer.' He made it sound as though he knew something I didn't: as though he'd seen bachelors perish in agony as a direct consequence of their singleness. 'My father says marriage is *impossible* and *unavoidable*.' Later he modified his advice. 'Get married, sir – but marry a man.' 'Good heavens – what sort of suggestion is that?' 'You see, if you marry a man, you won't have a baby.' 'Oh.' Those eyelashes busily at work. 'Do you *set any store* by my advice, sir? You ought to, you know. My father is a very well-known doctor. Did you know that? And so is my mother. They are all doctors in my house. But I shan't be one. I don't like whisky, you see.'

He was clever with a pencil, with paint and scissors. Early that term he made a gift to the staffroom: a sheet of grey paper, folded and cut into the shape of a house. One half was the exterior, windows and doors cut in it: the other, the interior, was queerly and attractively hazy, with whisky and soda on a dining room table, and a neglected tap pouring a flood of white-painted water on to the bathroom floor. This, he explained, was the veritable Musk household: and the model was somehow yet another item in his sequence of charming treacheries.

Rosie, I would tell myself, was a most extraordinary mirror in which mother and father could be seen in terms of ingenuous parody. That silkiest of voices, those eyelashes used with such deliberate coquetry – these were tricks surely borrowed from his mother. For those disconcertingly mature turns of speech he must be referring back to his father. He was much given, for example, to the ejaculations: 'Great Scott!' and 'Dammit!' As soon as he was confident of my mildness, as quickly happened, the phrase when addressed to me became: 'Dammit, *man*!' He would watch as I put a cross against one of his sums: 'Dammit, man!' he'd cry. 'What's wrong with it?' But he was not greatly interested in arithmetic. He would, usually, have one of his vaguely shady propositions to make to me, there in the middle of a lesson.

'Sir!' it was once. 'Why do you *insist* that I play football? It is *tedious*, you know! Can't you let the Grocer and me just . . . walk about and talk? Oh, go *on*!'

The Grocer was Paul Gross, Musk's bosom friend, now adding his smiles from the body of the class to Rosie's purring persuasions.

'Oh, such nonsense, Rosie . . .' My voice as gruff as I could make it.

'If only you'd do that, sir,' he persisted, laying a finger on one of my knuckles and lightly rotating it, 'the Grocer and I would be your *devoted slaves* for ever! Honest!'

'An extraordinary proposal, Musk,' I said, 'and this second sum is just as hopelessly wrong as the first.'

'Great Scott, man,' he murmured. 'And the third will be just as hopelessly wrong as the second.' He was right about that.

Bosom friend was perfectly the phrase for the Grocer. He and Musk went everywhere arm-in-arm, exchanging elegancies. I found myself obliged to think of them in French: *petits hommes de sentiment*. The Grocer carried with him at all times a tin box which contained photos of mother, father, two sisters and his dog. He caused Mr Diamond curious rage once with his reply to my colleague's manly inquiry at assembly: 'What are you hugging there then, lad?' The Grocer looked at Mr Diamond with enormous eyes and declared: 'Oh sir – my *heart* – my *life*!' 'I find some of them rather disgusting, you know,' Mr Diamond told the staffroom. '*Pansies* is a word that meets the case, if you ask me.' 'Ah, but such a charming flower,' Harrod Parker murmured to the plaster blossoms on the staffroom ceiling.

Sophisticated sentimentalists, aged ten – Rosie and the Grocer. Footballers they certainly were not. The Grocer claimed, indeed – as if it were some conventional alternative – to be a botanist. In practice this meant that he collected vegetable matter with no evident discrimination. Beyond grass, there was not much matter of the kind on the football ground. But that was a lack that stimulated rather than defeated the Grocer. He would stray from the game into such roughage as there was, along the margins of the pitch, and would make a great thing of staring searchingly on the ground. If I called, 'Oh, for goodness sake, Gross, you're supposed to be a defender', he would look up, fix me with the saddest eye and say: 'I'm on the track, sir, of something that might turn out to be rather important.' 'What sort of importance?' I once rashly asked, trotting past with my whistle. 'Oh sir,' said Rosie, speaking for his friend, 'important to the World of Living Things and to God's Whole Creation.' 'Rubbish!' I cried. 'Claptrap!' At that moment I was kicked savagely on an ankle and turned to find one of the team captains glaring at me. 'Sir,' he cried, 'a foul . . . and you weren't even looking!' 'Sir's never looking when we need him,' someone called, and suddenly I was deeply unpopular. As I prepared to resist the mob, I caught Rosie's eye: he had contrived to fill it with the most liquid expression of censure.

The dispute over, the game smoulderingly resumed, I looked round and saw that Rosie and the Grocer were now some distance off, peering at the ground, hand shamelessly in hand.

There was not to be much football that term, as it happened. At the end of January the most appalling winter of the century was to descend and turn the world to shuddering iron. In respect of football only, I was grateful to that savage weather when it came.

I still had my junior game, and Mrs Cakebread remained my

companion. She persisted in treating my ignorance of the game as a fine and sensitive refusal to interfere with the boys' enjoyment.

'What a good thing you're not one of those masters who insist on everything being correct,' she'd say. 'You can't, with little ones like these, can you?' I knew she was too honest to mean the opposite of what she said: but I couldn't help wondering if she was hinting at some anxiety . . . consoling herself for a chaos I had no power to avert. I continued to read through the rules of the game, from time to time, with no increase of understanding. It was like reading a set of ground rules for my relationship with Rose-M. No doubt these could have been formulated; but I knew I should have been unable to work from them to the actual complexities of our encounters. Still, it seemed bad to have always this hopeless, if extremely energetic, muddle of boys kicking the ball into one another's stomachs. Claims in respect of alleged fearful abdominal injury were common features of my games.

My senior game was at times happy to proceed in its own way: at other times, furious with my unhelpfulness. 'Sir,' I was asked at last, 'why don't you tell us where we're wrong?' I began nervously to do this: or rather, to utter loud cries of recommendation or dissuasion which had, to my ear, roughly the right sound. This new activity of mine seemed to increase the general enjoyment of the game. I even began to believe in the relevance of these shouts and urgings. The only times when I was overcome by bashfulness occurred when some passing workman stopped and peered over the fence into the ground. There were bad days when someone would do this for a quarter of an hour at a time. How odd it was, I thought, this English lust for football, that caused a grown man to stop and watch intently a game played by little boys of eight, nine or ten. At such moments, I became very self-conscious indeed, and would blur and mutter those exhortations out of which, at other times, I reckoned safely to compose my refereeship.

It remained one of my greatest fears: being unmasked, as a pretender to the position of referee and coach, by some such passerby, to whom the misinstruction in football of small British boys would be a hanging matter.

2

It was towards the end of January that our traumatic winter really began. There was a day when the snow fell with a sort of idleness, a twist and flurry that was almost weary: it was caught in great sideways and upward sighings of air, deadly chill, that seemed capable of returning it to the sky it came from. But still it fell: and the temperature with it, to zero and then below. By the following day the snow had gained a fearful confidence, and came down in blinding masses, now with the character of pure ice. The ground became a horribly thick sluggish carpet that squeaked and groaned as we laboured across it. Falsely a weather forecast promised that the temperature might 'rise towards freezing point'. Buses were lucky and unlikely acccidents. Coal disappeared; gas followed it. School lunches, for the dwindling number of boys, were lukewarm. Mr Juniper appeared in an overcoat: a personal defeat he took hard. His revenge was to rearrange the timetable in quite an impressively unpractical fashion.

Mr Diamond was unsurprised by all this. He had expected nothing less from the election of a Labour government. 'They've cut the gas off now, y'see,' he pointed out. 'We shall grind to a halt. Everything will go. They simply don't know how to govern, y'see.' And he stared out of the staffroom window at the leftwing snow lying where Mr Attlee and his team had allowed it to accumulate, in ungentlemanly heaps.

I had lost touch with Rose-M altogether. Tom Randall's hints about the bakerboy, or the Baker boy, together with the renewed dismays of teaching, had seemed to thrust her away into some remote corner of life; I wasn't sure if I meant to leave her there and accept this fading of contact, or if I thought of her as shunted into some paradisal siding to which the clanking mainline course of things would at last return me. And now the weather had brought the affairs of The Under Thirties to a halt, so even that possibility of encounter was removed. I dreamed of a mocking Rose-M, slowly twirling on icy toecaps beyond a mountain of fallen snow; then her expression changed to one of patient adoration . . .

At times my heart stood still as it struck me that it was perhaps intolerable to treat in such a fashion a girl who'd been so kind and confiding. At other times it seemed only fair to offer her a chance (a month or two long) to recover from the precipitancies of our last evening together.

Weaving such uncertainties into my work, I continued my attempts to be a maths teacher. It was the worst boys who seemed to withstand the weather, as an obstacle to travel and a threat to health. The angels, the pleasant little fellows, were all laid low. Hazard and his friends looked perfectly capable of surviving the most atrocious elemental disasters that the Labour government might contrive.

I felt two things were happening to me as a teacher. I was close to being accepted as a natural part of the school background – as familiar as some table in the hall, kicked and cut. I was at the same time making a habit of my own chaotic and uncriticized style of teaching. I was beginning indeed to accept myself – my shouting, unstable self of the classroom, veering crazily between anger and amusement – as a part of nature. I tried to remain aware that when I set out to explain, too often I baffled. My explanations were like . . . oh, immense attempts to give an account of thousands of square miles of complicated country . . .

Of course! I was working in great blocks of explication, and that was nonsense! So I was embarking on long soliloquies; and naturally enough these were interrupted, and I grew sore at the interruptions! I must break up my teaching into tiny steps . . . a little explanation, a little practice: and then again, and again.

I felt cautiously more successful. But oh that nightmare of small sharp voices! No one who'd not taught could have any idea of the strain of having to regulate the affairs of so many excitable little boys!

As football and other sports became impossible in our frozen world, Harrod Parker suggested a twice-weekly blood-letting. 'While they're at prep,' he proposed in Mr Diamond's presence. 'A pint at a time. We might give an up to anyone volunteering to give a pint and a half.' 'Ha ha', Mr Diamond laughed, uneasily. 'I think we might have some letters from parents.' He patted Harrod Parker on the back and hurried off, as he always did from the neighbourhood of all but the broadest jokes.

The school was filling up again now it had become clear that the winter was not one you could see off with a few days in bed. The untapped energy of the boys grew greater daily. It appalled a new colleague of ours, Peter Nicholas.

Peter, on his way to Cambridge, was spending two terms in our company. There was some tradition of teaching in the family, and the theory was that he would dip a toe into the professional experience, to see if it was for him or not. It was, I suspected from the start, a quite perfunctory toe. Peter had no air of the teacher whatever. His reaction to life at The Vale was one of polite startlement. I'd say, perhaps: 'I'm afraid my class might have deafened yours this morning. My maths teaching seems to excite them rather surprisingly.' Peter would smile, darkly, and then duck his head as if to prevent the smile escaping into general circulation. 'You flatter me,' he'd say. 'The noise in my own room's too great for me to hear anything beyond it.'

Mr Diamond would find us laughing together in the staffroom. 'You young fellows brighten up the scene,' he would observe, complacently. 'You find so much to amuse you.' Mr Diamond was never one to waste such comments: he'd turn and call across to other members of the staff. 'These young fellows brighten up the scene, y'know.' Our colleagues would nod, politely. 'They find so much to chuckle about.'

The ghost of a thought that this was not a perfectly proper response to teaching would cross Mr Diamond's mind. 'And not at all a bad thing! By no means *altogether* a bad thing, to look on the lighter side.' Then his invariable final generalization, which often consisted of elevating a casual observation into a lifelong principle. 'I've always felt that looking on the lighter side is a thoroughly good thing. Thoroughly good thing!'

I regarded Peter Nicholas with some awe. It seemed a luxury beyond words, to be able to experiment in the most uncommitted way with teaching – to have a taste of it, in Mr Juniper's phrase. Oh, to be able to *taste* teaching – and then, like Peter, to screw up your eyes and splutter: and laugh a little at your own absence of enthusiasm. And your family laughed with you and said: 'Ah well, old chap – that's not it, then . . .' And off you went to other tastings, of other possible ways of life.

'Such a civilized arrangement,' I said once, enviously. Peter, whose nature it was to pursue accuracy of statement, ducked away from this, with his dark smile. 'Oh, that's to make too much of it,' he said. Mr Diamond caught us laughing. 'My goodness, you young fellows! You do enjoy yourselves,' he exclaimed.

From Mr Diamond, whose speech was an affable uproar, a series of stylized noises, Peter found himself constantly bound to duck away. As he did now. Mr Diamond said, with vast vagueness: 'My goodness – what it is to be young!' Then, with no change of tone: 'My hat, it's snowing!'

Only someone with Mr Diamond's passion for pinning down the obvious would have commented on a commonplace blizzard. The world had become a prison of snow: we'd walked for weeks on thick floors of ice. They were floors of a glassy unevenness. Wireless programmes shrank: the Third Programme vanished. Every day brought some disappearance. Now the street lights were gone; now the weekly magazines. We collected amazing statistics of gloom: that, for example, in the month of February the sky was free of cloud for six minutes.

I worked for days on a letter to Rose-M. It so preoccupied me that I was in danger of writing phrases from it on the blackboard, as a startling element in, say, Upper Four's maths. It was to express serene love, a profound scepticism as to all amorous activity, a cool acceptance of the long gap between meetings, a terrified guilt in respect of the same. One evening I made a fair copy of the latest version and compelled myself to post it. Then I held my breath, for days on end.

It was about this time that, suddenly, appallingly, all the boys were calling me Gilbert.

I'd read a story to Lower Five in which there was a character of this name. There seemed to be an instant feeling that to address me by it was perfectly to account for me. I was, somehow, pure Gilbert. 'Hi, Gilbert!' boys would call. I didn't recognize the danger; I smiled – feeling that I was being broad-minded, of course, not narrowly given to offence, and so on. Within days a casual joke had become an outrage. Everywhere and insistently and in impossible circumstances I was now Gilbert.

It was my lunch table that made the most of it – now *Gilbert's* table.

Cheetham was the spark that kept them burning. His manner was a fusion of the meekest respect and the wildest insolence. His view of teachers was that the dignity they set out to maintain could in every case be destroyed by the uncovering of a few squalid facts. Outstanding among these was one's Christian name. Anyone whose Christian name was widely known, it went without saying, was a ruined man. In my case, the collapse that would flow from such a discovery had been overtaken, one might have thought, by the consequences of my nickname. I was surely as conclusively ruined as even Cheetham could wish. But there was no limit to his oddly goodnatured malice. When he was moving in for a real attack on a reputation, he'd perform a war dance round his victim. I'd been the centre of one of these about this time: Cheetham crying, 'I'm opening a file on Gilbert!' He'd smiled at me so eagerly, given me in his circlings so many nudges with the elbow, that I'd felt obliged in my turn to smile, nervously. It was, after all, like the announcement of the granting of some crazy honour.

The first entry in my file had been based on Cheetham's fancied discovery that I was married. Marriage, of course, was a mockable weakness, to begin with: but he'd also established, to his entire satisfaction, that my wife was called Beatrice. It was an extra dimension of disgrace, in his view, that this should be her name: an attitude strengthened by the way he pronounced it. To him, the lady was Beet-riss. Now, when we met, he would prance round me in a state of high excitement, crying: 'Gilbert's wife's called Beet-riss! Gilbert's wife's called Beet-riss!' It was a style of proposition to which no useful answer suggested itself. I'd frown, irritably, filled with a helpless impulse which, when I tried to give it a name, seemed to amount to a wish that schoolmasters could institute, against eleven-year-old schoolboys, massive actions for slander.

Especially did I wish this in Cheetham's case, because of what had once followed from the fact that his father was a professor of language studies. 'Oh, Gilbert, sir,' Cheetham had cried at lunch. 'Gilbert, sir, I told my father how you taught us to parse, and he said you ought to be sacked.'

'Said Gilbert ought to be sacked?' said Nightingale.

'The whole staff should be sacked,' said Rider-Smith. 'A repulsive lot.'

'Really, sir,' said Cheetham. 'Really, Gilbert. He said you weren't qualified.'

'Why pick on Gilbert?' said Nightingale. 'They're all like it.'

'Old Snogger!'

'Pisspot!'

Perhaps they *were* all like it: but at least Mr Proust, Geography and French, I thought, didn't get called 'Pisspot' to his face.

Oh, this weak amiability of mine! In any interval in the torment provided for me by some of my classes, I'd be so benign! In fact, much of my original pure fear of teaching had faded, but this great weakness remained: my inability to resist boyish silliness, with its face-screwing pantomime, its incongruous lapses into innocence. A quite passable attempt at control would be ruined by the irrepressible grin that would twist my lips, however I sought to tighten them.

Why could I not acquire a kind of sensible and serviceable beast-liness? Instead I lurched from warmth of feeling and great amusement to . . . a nervous quarrelling with my pupils! I bickered with them at best, raved at them at worst, in an untidy nerve-racked fashion.

It was made no better, of course (and as I waited for a reply to my letter, it was made much worse), by my agonies over Rose-M. Being in love and learning to be a teacher were not compatible activities. I should, I thought at times, have been able to claim leave of absence on National Health. Lovesickness – or simply amorous uncertainty – was disabling enough for that.

My lunch table, under the prompting of Cheetham, produced a newspaper. It was on a day when suddenly, all over the shivering school, small brass tops had appeared – had been set spinning on desks and floors and every sort of surface. It was like being attacked by metal locusts. There had been, all round, a great swatting and confiscation – and at any moment, we all understood, Mr Diamond would leap to apoplectic feet and make the possession of such things a capital matter. Meanwhile, at my table, the little tops twirled and tinkled among the plates, set spinning by no visible hand. In answer to my protests, Cheetham, with the sweetest of smiles, presented me with the first copy of *The Gilbert Gazette*.

3

'What', wrote Rose-M, 'should a poor girl think when she hears nothing for weeks on end from a man who once told her he'd die without her? You wrote a lovely letter but I didn't understand a word of it. However, I am trying to forget my *long cold rage* and suggest you meet me outside the parish church at eight p.m. on Friday. And I warn you I shan't wait more than a month.'

It was the longest and cruellest day I'd ever known, that Friday. The school had never been colder. I couldn't bear the touch of chalk on my numbed skin: my tongue was as big as a fish, and I roared at my classes in a slurred way. I reflected that I couldn't remember what the bare sky looked like. A boy accused me of incoherence of teaching: 'You chop and change,' he said. And indeed I knew that, in maths especially, I had no overall plan: I lived from day to day, trying to cram everything in. Doing fractions, I felt suddenly guilty about decimals: having switched to these, I remembered the existence of square roots.

After lunch I was put in charge of Upper Six prep. This was a likeable form, dominated by a boy who was pure clown. Saint, as ironically his name was, had no need of makeup. His nose was a red bulb; his mouth an enormous upturned arc, which at a second's notice could become an enormous arc turned down. He was clearly and yet invisibly in charge of the chatting, humming and the asking of absurd questions with which the prep began. Soon Saint took over openly. He began to crack jokes: at least, they had the shape and sound of jokes, though my anger and the laughter of the other boys made them incomprehensible to me. Hysteria filled the room. My anger was the sharper because I knew that, within fair limits, I could prevent the outbreak of spectacular disorder. It wasn't fair, surely – it wasn't fair! And I liked Saint, anyway – I positively liked that cheery face, so readily besotted with amusement. 'If you knew how easy it was to make jokes, you wouldn't do it!' I roared. There was general delight at that. Saint stepped up his production of bright comment. A voice cried: 'This is a wonderful prep!' 'Have you learned anything?' inquired another. Wildly I took my cue. 'You can learn whatever it is you have to learn tomorrow after lunch. You will stay behind in the hall and do what you are supposed to be doing now.' It was, judging by the reception given to it, the best joke of the afternoon. Words suddenly poured out of me.

'Do you really think it funny? I think it ill-mannered! It's very easy for you to sit there making jokes. But is it fair? I could give you detentions, but what's the point of that? Well, you have the power! You've chosen the easy thing – very well! Carry on! Use your power!'

At least I was warm at last – fairly hot with vexation. And suddenly there was silence. It was absolute, it was exemplary. There was not a murmur. For the last quarter of an hour they bent over their work, grave-faced. I felt the uneasiness and incredulity of someone who has halted a battle with a cry of protest. Even guilt moved within me.

Had it been right to stifle all that gay energy? I was terrified of making a noise myself.

When the bell went I half-expected a disgusted demonstration. Instead the captain of the form rose and said: 'We apologize for behaving like that. We're sorry.' 'Oh good heavens,' I said. I managed to prevent myself from adding: 'It's I who should apologize'. Saint said, with a ghost of his natural grin: 'We can't resist a little ill-mannered humour, you know.' We bowed out of each other's presence.

It was in a tangle of recollections of this scene, and of pure terror of the heart, that I approached the parish church a few minutes before eight o'clock. Rose-M was already there, on the bleak white pavement, in her coat of golden fur. She held up her face for a kiss. 'What an achievement!' she cried, glancing up at the church clock.

Looking back, I marvel at Rose-M's forbearance and obstinacy. She had become entangled with a monster. There was a sense – it was a matter of touching, teasing, of soft things said and charming things done – in which what happened between us was pure delight. But as I struggled to be absorbed by her, I struggled also to escape. The difference between one of our meetings and the next was the difference between two tides. Now it would be all sharp-edged rocks and the beach's desolation: next time it would be the full swelling sea.

That evening it was first one and then the other. She tucked her hand into the crook of my arm, she clung on. My own hand hung awkwardly, not finding hers. She laid her head on my shoulder. Still I was rigid, helplessly distant. In my head a small furious voice asked: Why can't you simply pay her the attentions a lover should? Ach – be easy, be natural! Be properly and gratefully delighted!

She said: 'Where are you? Where have you gone? Oh, why can't you take things as they come?'

Through the High Street a few figures, bent against the cold, shuffled along the glacier of the pavement. The unevenness had been made worse by intermittent attempts to clear the frozen snow. We went up and down, from one lumpy level to another.

'The Baker boy? Oh, was that Tom Randall gossiping? . . . How can I tell you? . . . You see, you brood on things so much – I'm afraid of telling you anything, for what you'll make of it. Well, he's Tony Baker, he's the wonder boy, he's the wizard airman – he was a very good fighter pilot, and he has all sorts of medals. All the girls . . . Oh, you see! You're working on it, already! I don't know that I even like him. He's very conceited. Not at all like you . . . although . . .' She laughed. 'But look here, who am I walking along this horrible pavement with, on this bitter evening! Tell me that!'

Then: 'Oh, let's go home! They're all out. You need thawing –

you certainly do need thawing out and warming up! Now, I'm very good at that.'

She captured my hand with her own valiant one: then encircled my ungracious waist, drew herself close to my miserable woodenness.

'You're coming home and you're going to tell me about teaching and I'm going to tell you about dancing. Oh, my dear, I think I'm a bad dancer! I've done some bad things lately – Cheer up! – some bad things *as a dancer*!'

We were on the floor in the neighbourhood of that gleaming piano. The sea was flowing back, drowning that stony beach under its smooth easy water. I seemed to be eating her hair. She was wholly edible. For a moment, I'd seen that my prime fascination for her was my perfect unsuitability. 'I love you because you think. But when you think, you make me anxious.' Now, on the floor, all thinking went under the sea, forgotten among the submerged rocks. I touched her thighs and couldn't for the life of me understand why such indisputable pleasure – oh, and what would follow from it, in unimaginable due course – could not be made a means of uniting our dissimilar natures, habits, wishes . . .

Of course, I thought, making my way dizzily home through the frozen midnight – of course, I must fix things, we must . . . become *engaged*. We must be brisk and practical. Between mistrust, jealousy, sexual inexperience, general uncertainty, I'd lost all ability to steer a calculated course. I simply didn't know enough about ordinary, brisk, practical things. There must be simple instructions, somewhere, for becoming . . . *affianced*. The thing was to be quite firm, in a perfectly commonplace way: there must be announcements, fixing of dates, contracts, public agreements . . .

'When,' she had asked again, 'are you going to sleep with me?' I must find out about that, too – *I must be practical in that direction*. It was like taking football – I must turn to the handbooks.

Only an idiot would start up again that invention of reasons for refusing the offer of those bright eyes, that vivid narrow face – the amazing softness of those thighs . . .

A few days later I was summoned for interview as a candidate for the teachers' emergency training scheme.

What, I wondered, would they be looking for? I imagined the model against which they might attempt to match me: obviously there'd be an element of the paragon in it, of the purposeful, bustling manager: a great dash of moral security: and, surely, perfect intellectual watertightness . . . I must not let them hear the gush of ignorance as it poured in past my defective plating. But I was very much afraid that they'd discover I had difficulties in distinguishing East from West, and had never overcome a certain vagueness in respect of square roots.

In fact, they asked me why I had chosen to mark time before training by teaching in a private rather than a State school.

I outlined clumsily, with hopeless bursts of unshared laughter, my tendency not to determine my path by such logic. 'I think my experience may not be wholly – ah – irrelevant,' I ventured, not believing a word of it. For I was shattered by a sudden certainty that to teach in a prep school was in some way to make oneself for ever unsuitable for teaching in the real world. Oh yes, the *real* world! Here were stern men and women to whom the existence of The Vale must seem – ah, such a frivolity! I was a pointless intruder from the luxurious margins of education. Education, indeed, might not be the word for what occurred at The Vale. Perhaps, instead, it was a sort of intellectual and social pampering? I was a fop, and a parasite, to whom all mainstreams were now forbidden.

A woman wearing a cherry-red hat seemed to be winking at me. Or was ferocious disapproval causing her a curious kind of difficulty with an eyelid?

There were questions about my failure in Higher School Certificate. I told, excitably desperate, the story of my disaster with a vital Latin exam. I had turned up to take that in the afternoon: a mistake, since it had taken place in the morning. I did not tell them of the uncertainty I'd felt ever since. Had I genuinely misread the examination timetable, or had my unconscious, with what must seem classical obedience to Freudian principles, sought to protect me from the other sort of disaster that would have followed from my actually taking the exam?

I sat, flushed, feeling foolish, and smiled at this admirable panel of undeceivable persons, who'd exposed my fatal inadequacies within a matter of minutes . . .

There followed a medical exam. The doctor listened to my heart and then wrote a frowning essay on the form in front of him. Even my heart, it seemed, was not a teacher's.

As I left the building, I found myself wondering if they'd divined that I was paltering with a young woman of unserious character. Yes, it was probably well within the power of their professional instinct to lay that bare, alongside all my other shames.

4

Early in March the sun shone for an hour or so. The tired ice gleamed under it.

I'd been reading John Richard Green's *A Short History of the English*

People, largely on buses travelling gingerly on the road between my home and the school. I supposed it was a very much out-of-date, romantic history. I think I loved it for that reason. It suggested a sequence of historical weathers – darkness and storms, and then bursts of pure human sunshine. Green's account of the Reformation made me, an absurd usher reading him on trolleybuses on my way to and from a prep school in 1947 – it made me enormously happy, as if Erasmus and Sir Thomas More were . . . uncles of mine: certainly persons I might encounter round life's next corner. In that bitter winter, full of the acidity of postwar sentiment, I was glad of this notion, however romantic, that history might have springs and summers, flowerings and even holidays of the spirit. For a time I thought of Rose-M as . . . oh, how absurd it was! . . . a species of Reformation lady. She sat in the sunlight and worked at . . . a tapestry, perhaps? We exchanged, in this vision of mine, buoyant aphorisms. The historical facts in Green's narrative, the very dates, had the quality of . . . well, of the disembodied choirs that struck up at sticky moments in bad films! Oh, but there was curious joy, reading an out-of-date history of England during those icy months . . .

And that moment of sunshine, early in March, woke helpless longings in me: fed by the chapters in Green on the New Learning – so full of a sense of sweetness, of world-renewal, tolerance, appetite. I wanted to be some brown, bearded vagabond wandering through woods.

Instead, I was an usher – impatient, as we all were, for the postwar world to take a shape, to escape from sour shadows. I was an usher reading 'The Hunting of the Snark' to Upper Four, some afternoon when we should have been playing football. Little Tudor kept creeping out to see the illustrations – I'd find him at my shoulder, breathing a noisy kind of discretion – 'Oh do sit down, Tudor', I'd beg, knowing that his tiptoeing to and fro might well awake a general restlessness in hearts less innocent. And he, agonized by his own conduct, but drawn by a compulsive need to see the pictures – little Tudor, whispering, 'Oh sir, I can't help it, and I'm being *very* quiet!' Hazard that afternoon was in some kind of eclipse; he and Dennis appeared to be asleep or dead. Nye had slipped forward till he was barely visible in his desk. Lightfoot ii was certainly studying a cricket handbook in the shadows at the back of the room.

Suddenly I felt the extent to which this school had become a known thing, amazingly familiar: and scores of little boys, habits of my eye and ear . . .

A group of sixth-formers, under the inspiration of the clownish Saint, established a form of insurance against punishment. It was perfectly calculated, actuarially: it paid out twopence for every 100 lines a boy might incur, and as much as 6d for a slippering, which was a rather light-hearted operation involving some actual wornout footwear of Mr Juniper's, and a shilling for a caning: with variations of one kind or another. Premiums differed, some boys being worse risks than others: one or two proudly uninsurable. It thrived for some weeks, this Pains and Penalties Insurance Inc. A reserve fund was raised by means of a prize crossword puzzle: entry cost sixpence, and the crossword was the smallest I'd ever seen. There were four squares only, 1 and 2 across and 1 and 2 down, and the clue was the same in all four cases: An exclamation. No one won a prize because the exclamation turned out to be ZZ, which Saint claimed was the cry uttered by a startled bee.

We had a new maths master with us, a Mr Coyle, a grey, efficient man, who let it be known that he thought we lacked a good basic arithmetic textbook. Mr Hollow, who'd had the school's maths in his hands for years, was himself accustomed to work from old Common Entrance papers. But he took Mr Coyle's point, and one day in March a new set of books appeared. Mr Hollow referred to this event with a hasty sort of embarrassed pride. Anyone who knew his job, he said, could teach from these. He dropped a copy in my lap.

The Sixpenny Arithmetic, paperbound, cost rather more than its title alleged. It had been about under that name, I gathered, since the days when a sixpence, as Mr Hollow himself would have put it, was a sixpence, and arithmetic was arithmetic. Behind it one imagined yet another *Sixpenny Arithmetic*, which invited calculations of the time a man might take to bath himself if, long before he could think even of taking his clothes off, he must work through a range of uncertainties as to sizes of tap, alternative plumbing systems, and the good sense or not of leaving the plug out. It was so phrased, in places, that one seemed to be in touch with some ancient, stiff, ceremonial approach to mathematics. Thus it would urge, loftily: 'Perform the following divisions.'

I'd thought that Stephen Leacock had laughed such books into the limbo of plain absurdities, but here they were, boldly represented in The Vale of 1947 by the *Sixpenny Arithmetic*, which was fat with exercises: with fraction sums, for example, that led to answers remote from natural occurrence or use. It was the world of 349/627: also of 3 acres, 5 sq. chains, 9 sq. rods, 567 sq. links.

It had, as companion, an answer book that I still think of as the most controversial printed work I have ever handled. It divided my pupils into the extraordinary few, whose calculations confirmed the book: and the many, whose work led to wrathful contradictions of it. Time and again I was required to demonstrate the justice of the official answer: time and time again, alas, following uneasy strings of computation across the page, I failed to do so.

The author of the *Sixpenny Arithmetic* was not alone in causing my charges to doubt the ordinary good sense of mathematics. I was diligent in support of him. One of my best contributory strokes occurred when I began geometry with Lower Four. They were hostile to the entire notion of a theorem. Sane people did not encourage such suppositions as theorems were based on. I had never been so unpopular. Out of the expensive rationality of their schooling I stepped, urging them to adopt certain ridiculous mental postures and to express this or that ludicrous curiosity. Who could be interested in making an issue of the character of a straight line? Who would wish to rummage about in the simple certitudes of the circle? My first lesson was received as a frank piece of insanity. Catching my eye, boys positively shook their heads. There was a general atmosphere of melancholy. Under the strain, Gilbert had cracked.

I recovered from all this by pure accident. It was now time to do some geometrical drawing; so I encouraged Lower Four to invest in sets of instruments. There was some grumbling about this, allied (with no apparent sense of inconsistency) to a great deal of self-importance. Having to buy a geometry set certainly constituted a moment of initiation. Possessor of such a set, you could no longer be a baby. It ranked as a sort of moustache. Jonathan Honey said, carefully: 'I hope they're really necessary. That's my sweet ration for a month, that is!' Boys walked about holding geometry sets in unusual positions, all of a conspicuous kind. So for a while you could tell a member of Lower Four because he carried his geometry set in his hand, constantly, the hand being thrust unnaturally forward, inviting attention. For a time it was impossible to get them to agree to a period of mere arithmetic. Mathematics now consisted in the deployment of protractor, compass and set square. I worked hard to provide such a use of them, and soon felt I was outrunning the industry of Euclid himself.

But it was a good time for me, as a teacher. I had stumbled on to a rare vein of what, in the boys' eyes, was simple commonsense in the mathematical field. Drawing circles with a compass was splendid. The only dissentients were boys with whom, as it happened, I had a special sympathy. For them, the point of a compass would never stand still at the centre of the circle they sought to draw. All their straight lines were deformed by hiccups of measurement. No lines of theirs, intended to meet, ever did anything but race away from each other in the general direction of infinity. None of their lines, absolutely required to stay apart, could be prevented from the earliest of collisions. The exercise books of such boys were filled with the rubbery grey excrement of erasure.

Among the substitutes for games were walks to the great Common that spread across the brow of the borough. We'd go in crocodiles: and, given all that snow, it was like conducting parties of one's enemies to an unguarded ammunition dump. Back at school, senior members of the staff would be giving extra lessons: an essential operation of the private school industry. The hall would be full of boys polishing up their Latin, French, geometry: at 7s 6d an hour per boy. On the Common, there'd be Harrod Parker, Peter Nicholas, myself – at bay against an army of snowballers. I found self-defence difficult. The little Stewart brothers, Scots and solemn, had laid claim to my hands, of late, on all such expeditions. 'I say,' I'd protest. 'Let me make a snowball or two.' But they'd hang on. 'Sir,' one would drone. 'You see, when we go to the Highlands in August—' 'Well, the end of July, really,' the other would propose. '*Sometimes* July,' '*Always* July.' 'You could ask our mother, sir.' '*How* could sir ask our mother?' 'At Running-over.' 'Our mother never comes to Running-over.' '*Sometimes* she does.' The Stewarts were the most contrary of siblings: their observations of family life tallied in no respect. Meanwhile, I was reeling under the impact of snowballs that, given such oblivious anchors, I had no hope of avoiding. 'We love you, sir,' one Stewart informed me, matter-of-factly. I longed to ask them to demonstrate their love by digging me a quick, deep trench.

If, by some stroke, I evaded the Stewarts, I'd fall captive to, say, Salter and Raymond-Jones. Salter came from a musical family that was determined to make a violinist of him. But musical eminence was not little Salter's ambition, at all. For some reason, he'd taken one of the local cinemas under his wing. Having entered into an understanding with the manager, he collected weekly batches of leaflets announcing future programmes, and carried these around in a small battered attaché-case to which he had stuck a label with 'PROGRAMS' printed on it. He'd distribute them to staff, first, and then to boys. Mr Juniper had been known to express great tetchiness, finding Salter in the entrance hall of the senior school on a Monday morning, handing out his leaflets. But there was no ready heading under which this could be defined as an offence. Salter's conversation, if he imprisoned a hand of mine, was coloured by the vocabulary of these leaflets. 'The film of the century, sir, and you must see it!' 'Sir – two desperate men fighting for the love of a beautiful, *dangerous* woman!' His gift, at the age of ten, was clearly that of a born sandwich-board-man. I thought that behind all this might lie the wish to leave as little room as possible in his head for glum thoughts about the violin and the problems of playing it to the satisfaction of his teacher and his ambitious parents.

Raymond-Jones was a boy given to helpless noisiness. He had too many teeth, it seemed, and these were constantly under constraint from one variety or other of brace. He was innocently compelled to say whatever came into his head – at the top of his voice: to which the current brace would give a drunken quality. 'Sir', he'd shout tipsily, 'Gilbert, sir! – Mr Parker's trousers are too big for his – Oh, sir,

you're cross! But they *are*! His—' 'Raymond-Jones – *please*!' 'Oh sir' –
an uncontrollable series of grins alternating with expressions of intense
alarm. 'I can't help it. You were so gentle with us in the juniors – I
really don't seem to be able to help it. I was born like it.' 'I don't
think you should talk disrespectfully about Mr Parker's trousers.'
There would be a gasping, grinning interval of silence. Then: 'The
new matron . . . her dresses are – They show you a lot, sir! Oh sir,
I can't help it!'

The new matron was young, coolly bright of mind, and certainly
given to wearing unmatronly dresses. She had a deep white bosom;
I was aware of being no more chaste in my observations than little
Raymond-Jones. I'd said once to Peter Nicholas, out of my obsession
with the agonies of marital choice, that I found myself wondering what
it would be like to be Miss Fuller's fiancé. He was serving with the
Army in occupied Germany: Miss Fuller would be with us only for a
year, when he'd be demobbed and they'd set up home together. 'At
least,' said Peter, 'one would be certain of having an intelligent
companion.' I winced – thinking of Rose-M. We'd had an edgy Saturday afternoon, walking in the town. I'd thought it would be a tender
occasion – I was to help her with her shopping. Oh, a step towards the
sweetest ordinariness of association: near-domesticity. I imagined her
with a rather pretty basket hooked over her arm. It wasn't like that, at
all. We'd started badly when she'd told me of a recent visit to the
theatre. 'Oh, my dear, what a play! – it *stinks*!' 'You mean,' I said
uneasily, 'that in your view it stinks.' 'Oh no. All of us in our party
thought it *really* stank!' 'But in what ways–?' 'Oh, it was – Oh, it *stank*!'
I waited for more information: but she was absorbed in a shop window.
'Well – it's a thumbnail criticism, certainly,' I said. She frowned at the
display that had caught her eye. 'Every one of those dresses would be
so *fattening*, don't you think?'

Outside a men's outfitters a placard cried: 'Come to the Practical
Tailors.' 'Who, then,' I mused, 'are the *unpractical* tailors?' Rose-M
reacted as though I were subjecting her to some brutally clever quiz.
'You tell me,' she said.

Later there'd been an hour or so under the lee of that huge piano . . .
That had been, in its sighing and smiling fashion, a period of real
tenderness: again we'd drifted into making light of our differences.
'I think you're the nicest person I've ever got tangled with on the floor.
But—' 'What hateful *but* is that?' 'But when are we going to try a bed,
instead?' I made the foolish face of a man who has done something
about *that*, oh yes, and is waiting for replies, supplies – something of
the kind. The matter's in hand. Meanwhile—

Meanwhile I thought of Miss Fuller, and a recent discussion of
Shakespeare's history plays I'd had with her and her deep, snowy
bosom.

Snow! At the beginning of March there was the promise of a thaw. It was ended by the wildest blizzard yet. Stinging storms of sleet were blown in waves and vicious spirals across the roads and back into the air. I waited an hour for a trolleybus to take me home.

The conservatism of The Vale's staff had deepened during those weeks. It was as though the cruel weather were making a party political broadcast. They nodded at it, deeply in agreement with such icy exposure of socialist fallacy.

I felt politically marooned: as when over staffroom tea Mr Juniper inquired about the Minister of Education. 'Not an educated person, I imagine? Self-educated, I assume.' His tone was not sharp or hostile – it was rather the tone of a man who discusses the baffling ways of total aliens. Mr Beesley said: 'Oh come, sir! An educated person for the Ministry of Education? You'll be expecting next a Foreign Secretary with a grasp of foreign affairs.' 'Or a Prime Minister,' growled Mr Raison from his armchair, 'who has some quality of primeness about him.'

In fact, public dejection had become very deep. Grumbling had us all in its grip. I thought how sad it was that the doggedness of wartime had been allowed to slip away now that there'd been a change of enemies. Now we were faced by the consequences of a monstrously exhausting struggle, allied to a damnable winter for which no earthly agent could be blamed. Surely what was needed, and what it couldn't be impossible to create, was an enlargement of the general imagination, so that instead of sulking under discomforts we were possessed by a belligerent comprehension of our plight? If the government was to be blamed, it was for its failure to cultivate that imagination.

At which point, with the agitations of term-end close at hand – the making of reports, the preparation of final holocausts of marking and great ultimate heaps of ups and downs – I collapsed. I was pole-axed by what might have been the flu, basically, but was also, I thought, as I lay shuddering and comfortless in bed, an overdose of emotional uncertainty coupled with grievous doubt about my occupation. What *was* I doing as a teacher? What was I doing in the fastidious conserva-tive world of The Vale? As the war receded, all that long paralysis of ordinary aims and wishes, the assumption of the role of peacetime citizen was exhilarating but deeply disturbing. One had the sensation of growing too fast – worse, that of not knowing in what direction one might best set out to grow. The sense of alternative destinies unpursued was terrifying.

The question was not only: Did I want to be a teacher? It was also: Ought I to be a teacher? Was I, with my stammering procedures, doing serious harm to the small boys in my charge?

I had nightmare after nightmare as the sick days went by. In a common one I was being married to someone I'd never even heard of.

She was a glum girl – the people around me in the dream were desperately trying to remember her name – and she stood foursquare and hopelessly plain and unlively, waiting for me at the altar.

I dreamed of appealing to Peter Nicholas. 'I'm in this awful fix! There she is and I – I simply don't want to go through with it!'

The duck of the head, the curious hesitation with which Peter addressed himself to almost any proposition. He was so anxious to catch the hidden note of truth buried in the inaccuracies of all our speech. 'Well, I really think you must give it a try. See if it's you. I suspect that it isn't.'

No, I thought in the middle of my dream. That's not about my marrying – that's about his attitude to teaching. Peter is going to make sure, if he can, that he gets his life right. I am doomed by my blundering character to get it hopelessly wrong.

Peter wrote to me about the traditional end-of-term gym display. The prizes were to be awarded by a famous wartime general, now deeply involved in the puzzling animosities of peace. Mr Juniper had been delighted by the great man's agreement to come. The display began without a sign of him. The staff had been sorely troubled. No one enjoyed the thought of a disappointed Mr Juniper. There was something boyish in him that took dismays very hard. A phone message came at last – the general would be arriving late. Mr Juniper made the announcement in a speech glowing with relief. We must not, he now felt free to say, expect men on whom the fate of the world depended to be punctual in their minor engagements.

'How characteristic of the Head,' Peter wrote, 'to assume that only an imminent world war could keep anyone from The Vale's gym display.'

Perhaps it was on the wave of this relief that Mr Juniper himself wrote to say that I must not dream of returning that term. 'As you know, I usually expect my young men to remain in good health – it's a matter largely of keeping the lungs full of fresh air and standing straight. But it's been a bad winter and we cannot always be perfect. Get well and enjoy the holiday, and we shall look forward to seeing you next term.'

I sank beneath the blankets and let the raging tail of the winter pass over me. I stirred myself only to read a letter from Rose-M – 'Are you looking forward to the summer? I am! The Under Thirties are proposing a *weekend* visit in June to *Brighton*. To see the Pavilion, etc. Will you come – to see the Pavilion, etc? I do miss our adventures underneath the piano.' I stirred again to read a letter from the Ministry of Education, which informed me that I'd been accepted for the emergency training scheme for teachers. Details of allocation to a college would be provided when they were settled.

5

You'd never have guessed, that May, that the world had ever known a winter. Sunshine was a whole new land to live in. The streets were suddenly full of ripe young women. Even cubbing became – at its edges, at any rate – delectable.

We took our packs, in their tipsy green caps, up to the common – from the very beginning of the new term this was possible. Miss Frome always had the firmest of programmes for such an occasion. There'd be the things we'd do together, intricate trackings and games that might be summarized as: How They Brought the Good News from That Bush over There to This Tree over Here (*not that one, Tudor, you ridiculously dreamy boy! Oh dear!* There would be palavers: which for me amounted to the ordeal of trying to keep a straight face when surrounded by a ring of grinning boys. Even more disgracefully dreamy than little Tudor, I'd easily lose touch with the brisknesses of such a programme. There'd be a team race, and the entire justice of the event would depend on my watching the proximity of toecaps to a line made of coloured bands stretching on the grass; and I'd be far away, fondling Rose-M with a wholly theoretical freedom, and suddenly Miss Frome would be saying: 'Well, we can count on Mr Blishen for a verdict on that! Mr Blishen! – we are all counting on you, you know!' The bedroom in my head would brutally melt, and I'd be back among the cubs of Tawny Pack, on the beaming Common.

Or there'd be some game involving dispersal, and I'd be sent on a tour of inspection: to discover that for every glade full of bickering cubs there'd be another containing some splendid young woman, turning her knees up to the fortunate sun. I'd come back to Miss Frome, half expecting one of her sharpnesses: 'Look, old chap, do get that look of *lust* out of your eyes, and try the effect of a good hard trot up to the top of the hill. I'll give you a timing, if you like.'

And there were so many badges being sought after by different boys. Lightfoot ii might come bursting out of a bush claiming to have qualified as an expert on . . . twigs, birds, animal droppings. Someone else carrying a teapot and a portable stove would be hoping – irritably, being so burdened on so hot a day – to qualify for a badge given to those who succeeded in making cups of tea in prescribed conditions of near-impossibility. I often thought – candidates permitting me to overhear soliloquies Miss Frome was shielded from – that a badge might well have been offered for verbal vigour under stress. 'Bloody damned bloody *bloody* teapot,' as I heard one of Lord Baden-Powell's smallest disciples exclaim, on such an afternoon.

Walking to school – among all those young women in their early morning hurry, who made a multicoloured, soft, flowing thing of the crowd – I'd realize how different my feelings were from those of two terms away, when the whole district had caused me terror. How menacingly elegant those large grey houses had seemed after five years spent in farmyards! And even about teaching, as that spring leapt into full summer, I now felt positively lighthearted.

The position of jester–cum–instructor to a crowd of little boys – well, it was a better job than many, surely.

Certainly the possibilities of distress had been increased by another curious piece of timetabling. I had, I thought, a tentative flair for teaching English: but I had only an odd lesson here and there in this role, largely in the junior school. I had no gift as a mathematician, and retained my work with the fourth year. As a geographer I was a plain idiot, and was now given two weekly periods of Geography with one of the fifth forms. My vagueness in this field was soon evident to the brighter spirits, who went out of their way to ask me to locate places which, if I said they were (on the strength of the names) in Hawaii, turned out to be in Australia, or *vice versa*. I was also made the target of an unnatural quantity of questions about the direction of the principal winds – no very comfortable experience for a man who had small difficulty in confusing the points of the compass.

It turned out that Geography, like History, was under Mr Diamond's ultimate command. I went to him for help with the syllabus. At the first hint of a question, Mr Diamond developed a rapid head of steam, and fairly vibrated with urgencies requiring his presence elsewhere. It was part of the professional manner of this man who was, I used to calculate, 99 per cent schoolmaster and 1 per cent private person. It was as if, surrounded for forty years by small inquisitive boys, he'd schooled himself to evade all questions beyond those strictly related to the Common Entrance examination. 'Well, young man,' he said, 'follow the book, follow the book! And now forgive me, dear chap! Trouble with Smith B. J. . . .'

The legend that Mr Diamond had perpetual trouble with Smith B. J. had been built up quite whimsically by the headmaster, abetted by Mr Diamond himself. Smith B. J. was in fact a large, slow, good-natured boy, whose progress through the school had caused constant concern. It had been like trying to push a rather lame elephant through a hundred yards sprint. Later in my teaching, elsewhere and in much less indulged circumstances, I met many Smith B. Js. Some of these having been constantly snapped and sneered at and even beaten for their Smith B. J.-ness, had become rather less than amiable. But at The Vale, Smith B. J. had been turned into a great fond jest. I thought it a cruel one, at times, but Smith B. J. smiled with apparently complete happiness through all the twists and turns of the joke.

Having his attention drawn to a particularly devilish problem set in some scholarship paper, Mr Diamond would not only say: 'That's something for Smith B. J.' but would at times actually have the boy sent for. 'Rees minor has a poser for you, lad! One of those you can do in your sleep!' Smith B. J. would stare at the problem, look more and more amazed, and scratch his head: and Mr Diamond would be delighted. His class, always anxious to please him, would express their own enormous amusement. 'Off you go, lad, then!' Mr Diamond would say, as complimentary as if Smith B. J. had exhibited masterly scholarship. And as he went out of the door: 'When you're in trouble, send for Smith B. J. Eh, lads!' Renewed delight all round.

At staff meetings, the joke arose when, in the long review of boys' hopes of reaching the goals among the public schools that they'd been set down for on their arrival at The Vale, or even earlier – when, in that sequence of groans and hopeful cries, Mr Juniper came to Smith B. J. His parents' aim was to get him into what I gathered was a very minor public school indeed. It was in the north, that in itself being a bad mark; and it had a blunt northern name, that might well have been the name of some nourishing pudding. I was shaken by the laughter that was earned by the mere mention of this school. 'Excuse me, sir,' Mr Diamond had said at the staff meeting at the beginning of that summer term. He rubbed away at the tears on his cheeks. 'Ha, ha, yes,' was Mr Juniper's response. 'Ha, ha, yes. Well, gentlemen. Smith B. J.'s prospects . . .' 'Oh, my goodness,' Mr Diamond gasped, already holding his sides. Someone said: 'One doesn't know whether the school was founded with Smith B. J. in mind, or whether Smith B. J. . . .' Laughter swamped this apothegm. 'Gentlemen, gentlemen!' Mr Juniper had urged. 'We must not indulge ourselves! To sterner things! Will little Bolsher win a Winchester scholarship?'

That was the area of the school's work about which I felt only a mildly terrified mystification. Here was I, engaged in dubious fashion with the Thirds and Fourths – roped in for peripheral, reparable activity with one of the Fifths. All that took me nowhere near the main operations room of The Vale – seen as the setting for the very precise, very expert, very successful plotting of a campaign to get boys into the public schools. Some of my colleagues – with Mr Diamond, Mr Hollow and Mr Raisin at their head – were strict and seasoned strategists in this field. Some eccentricity and callowness of teaching could

127

be tolerated in the middle reaches. But, given what Mr Diamond called 'reasonable material', the grounding provided by the efficient ladies of the junior school was made good and eventually built upon by the formidable professionals who made up the bulk of the senior staff. The humming sounds of extra lessons with which the afternoon and early evening school was filled was the sound of an extremely capable operation, conducted by men who knew by heart twenty or thirty years of Common Entrance papers in their own subject. 'My goodness,' you'd hear Mr Diamond thundering inside his classroom, 'you're going to have trouble, lad, aren't you, with Question 3 in Part B of the second paper?'

'Well, gentlemen – *he*'s out of the window,' Mr Juniper would inform his staff. By which he meant that some child, unlikely to achieve the paradoxically named Common Entrance – it seemed only logical that it should be known instead as Uncommon Entrance – had been persuaded to leave the school.

It has to be said that usually a boy required some defect other than slowness of mind to qualify for ejection by way of Mr Juniper's window. Apart from Smith B. J., there were not a few slow children among us, to balance that brightness that made Peter Nicholas dread a period of geometry with Upper Six. 'They would make Bertrand Russell pant a bit, I believe,' he said of those high-flyers.

There was fat Sloper, for example, in Lower Four, simple, honest, always applying his hot, inky lips to my ear in order to whisper his answer (usually scandalously inaccurate) to a sum. Sloper seemed to believe there was something very deeply confidential about mathematics. He worked with an arm flung round his book – protecting his inaccuracies, one uneasily felt, from eyes more awesome than those of his classmates.

Once, my tired anger finding a near-random victim, I'd given Sloper a detention. His grief and despair were amazing. Weeping enormously, he fell on his knees and beat his breast – the only human being I've positively seen doing this. I hurriedly cancelled the catastrophe; but for the rest of the lesson the room was filled with his sobs, a heartbreaking decrescendo. I felt that even Herod might have scowled at me.

Then there was Radley, who would frown with nervous apology even as he entered a classroom, and begin at once to excuse himself for his slowness. He would attack himself hastily, before he could be attacked. 'I'm slow, sir. I don't seem to follow very easily. Oh, I'm sorry, sir – I'm such a fool!' I tried a score of ways, all vain, to reassure this little boy. The exotic Musk was a close and spiteful friend of his. 'Radley is *a pain in the neck*, sir! Oh, do stop *babbling* – man!' At times

I hardly knew what to do, between my longing to calm Radley and the need to nip Rosie's comments in the cruel bud.

How one worried to understand these little boys, to be just to them! In Upper Four there was Stent-Davis, who was one of those for whom Mr Juniper's window was waiting. He was not slow, but had a tangled mind; it was known that his home was unhappy, quarrelsome. His parents played some bitter game in which one or the other was always leaving for ever. It was a fair guess that Stent-Davis had rarely known a moment of emotional security. His clothes reflected his condition: everlastingly rumpled, torn. Coming once from a period of Religious Knowledge, Harrod Parker said: 'No doubt about it – Stent-Davis's work in RK is that rare thing, a completely original form of blasphemy.' Presented with any sum whatever, he'd embark on a sequence of purely private operations that would fill a quarter of an exercise book, and come at last to the most unexpected and knotty sort of wildly wrong answer. Simplicity was beyond him. He needed involution – an intricate, crabbed, private method of his own, which must be beyond his comprehension as it was beyond yours. 'I don't know,' he'd say smilingly, when begged to explain. 'It just came! and now it's gone again! You know how it is with me, sir . . . Yes, I do listen to your explanations. I listen very attentively. But somehow – when I begin – it comes to me – my own way of doing it. You see? But I really can't think now . . . I really can't . . . *retrace my steps*!' And ending always triumphantly with some elderly phrase of this order – he was an eleven-year-old with a curiously mature vocabulary – he would smile with the utmost kindness.

It was so with all his subjects. It was in this way that he produced in Latin lessons what Mr Raisin alleged was a form of Serbo-Croat: another twisted language of his own in French: and work in Geography that seemed to relate to the structure and behaviour of some other planet than this one. In Art he specialized in cramped daubs that caused pain even to Mrs Plenty, whose geniality covered every other kind of artistic product. Yet all this wrongness, this involved waywardness of working, was marked by a sort of eager courtesy, found particularly exasperating by such a blunt man as Mr Diamond.

Stent-Davis was also given to losing his equipment. Pens, rulers, books – all would have gone: his desk would be empty: there were, sir, intruders, marauders, strange light-fingered phantoms about the place who gave themselves up entirely to robbing him. It was odd, it was awkward – yes, it was exasperating; but what could one do? He would shrug, with unhappy charm.

Losing one's books, mislaying one's homework – commonplace boyish tricks! But the wholesaleness with which Stent-Davis operated raised him far above the commonplace. I grieved him at one point that summer term by storing in my desk a spare set of everything, ready for the moment when he declared his usual complete loss. When the time came, he hid his vexation under a pleasant chuckle. 'Sir, you've shown *great foresight*! I suppose you have to, with some-one so *strangely unlucky* as myself!' But next day they'd gone again. 'I don't know, sir!' he said, eyeing the class as though they were a mob of wizards he'd been unlucky enough to fall among. 'I just don't know!'

The Vale just didn't know, either. He was a boy to be sighed over, whose difficulties were clearly rooted outside the school. 'Really, sir – he'll have to go out of the window,' Mr Diamond would urge at staff meetings. Untouched by the quality of charm in the little boy's pale smile, Mr Diamond would bark at him at morning prayers: 'Write me fifty lines for smirking, lad!' The master on detention duty would groan, knowing that Stent-Davis loved being detained (loved not having to go home, we sometimes suspected), and could do very strange things with the apparent simplicity of fifty lines.

His idleness grew, became an outrage. One day he collected three detentions, and was reported to Mr Juniper to be 'otherwise dealt with'. This, at worst, meant one of Mr Juniper's slipperings. But in the study, faced with that mild weapon, Stent-Davis screamed with panic, anger – who knows with what backlog of despairs. He flew at Mr Juniper and bit him. The headmaster, unaccustomed to being bitten, marched the boy to the front door of the school and told him to go home. 'I never want to see you again!' he cried.

Stent-Davis ran off, weeping wildly. When Mr Juniper's anger had died, he remembered what the boy had sobbed as he flew down the front steps. 'My mother will kill herself! Oh dear, oh dear! – my mother will kill herself!' Mr Juniper phoned the boy's home to say he'd take Stent-Davis back after due apology. He reported the sequel to the staffroom.

'Well, his father says they'll try another school. It'll be the fourth or fifth, I believe.'

'I can't say I'm sorry, sir,' said Mr Diamond, comfortably. 'He's one we ought to be glad to have successfully shoved out of the window. Though he jumped through it himself, I suppose you could say.'

Mr Juniper showed no appreciation of the joke. 'I can't help wishing we'd been able to help that . . . puzzling little boy,' he said. Then he brightened. 'But it means I can take a very sharp fellow whose father came to see me today. They want to get him into Harrow, and there shouldn't be much difficulty about that.'

6

Gaps were opening up again between my meetings with Rose-M. She was busy, she said, with dancing tests and performances. There was an evening when we sat on a stile in fields close to her house and watched the evening star arrive and then others appear round a snow-white flake of moon. We held hands and simply watched the world darken about us – trees, grass, bushes shaking in a small wind. 'You're nice this evening,' she said. 'You could be perfectly nice you know. If you didn't struggle so much. If you tried to *accept* more. I wonder why you have to make yourself unhappy.' 'My dear girl,' I said, 'I really don't set out to be unhappy. I simply react to the situation.' 'Bugger your reactions,' said Rose-M, kissing me at once. 'Oh dear – it will take more than a kiss to stop you brooding over my coarse language.'

We seemed, that evening, to have come too close for any long separation to be possible. But days passed after that. I populated her silence with handsome men, a string of champion suitors: contemptuous disloyalties. The old fears, suspicions, discomforts returned. Then I ran into James. 'Saw Miss P the other night,' he said. 'Walking home from the bus, looking rather lonely. Quite wistful, I thought.' James added, with a touch of superiority, that he and the secretary of The Under Thirties had spent an agreeable day in the local woods recently. 'Discussing Haydn. And sometimes not discussing Haydn,' he explained, with a coyness that did not suit him.

I found then that I was simply grieving for Rose-M. Suddenly I felt that I had been driving away real affection. Love struck me like a sickness: I ached. There was for a while no comfort of body or mind.

Fool! And while this argument was going on in my head, for, against, for, against, she was to stand waiting patiently for the outcome?

'You detention master, sir?'

I nodded, placed the heavy detention book on the desk, and looked round at my penitential charges. They didn't look very unhappy. For some reason, detention at The Vale was often a gay affair: like a meeting of some unorthodox club. From outside the window came the sounds of snarling dispute: the boarders were playing cricket in the yard.

I'd done a little research in the matter of detention, lately. A third of the masters were responsible for two-thirds of the detentions inflicted. I was myself not the most assiduous punisher: Peter Nicholas had that honour. Mr Diamond was the sole member of staff whose initials appeared nowhere in the book. One saw that he would have his own ways of dealing with any offence that couldn't be met simply with one of his amazing denunciations.

'Naughty, sir,' said Musk, stroking my sleeve. 'I wasn't making a noise.' And indeed, looking into his unscrupulously liquid eyes, I saw that 'noise' was not a suitable description of the crime for which I myself had, that day, given him a detention. But how else could one categorize that silky disruption of routine, the suave anarchy in which Musk specialized?

'Do I *have* to write an essay on "The Dangers of Talking too Much"?' he sighed; and, without waiting for an answer, went away to do it.

'Learned my poem already. Hear me,' cried Bolton, of Upper Five, bounding up and thrusting a volume of verse into my hand. I looked in the detention book. 'Bolton. Shouting in class. Learn "On First Looking into Chapman's Homer",' I read. I shuddered. Overtaken by a desire to hear this sonnet recited, one would not have chosen Bolton as the performer. His prime qualities were those of a wild dog. He was always barking and bounding at you and sending you reeling.

'"Much have I something'ed in the what's-its-name of gold",' he now bawled, '"And many thingumabobs and what-nots seen."' He tried to look winsome, and barged me with his shoulder. 'Oh go on, sir. I've said it, haven't I?'

I recovered my balance. 'Come back when you know it,' I said.

'Now look,' said Grayson, of Lower Six. His formmaster, Mr Capper, said of Grayson that he'd surely win an Eton scholarship if Eton could be persuaded of the academic grandeur of a study of the British railway system. Grayson was one of several obsessives at The Vale, whose earnestness as scholars, alas, was inspired by fields of inquiry unknown to Common Entrance examiners. That hopelessly slow boy, Radley, for example, was extremely quick of mind, and impressively well-informed, in the matter of aeromodelling. I'd once, on an afternoon too wet for sport, set Upper Four debating the relative advantages of living in town and country. Radley's contribution was brief and passionate. The town, he said, was infinitely better if one wanted to buy model aircraft: but the country had the edge when it came to flying them. He confessed that, as a result of this paradox, his whole life plan was painfully uncertain.

Now Grayson dropped an exercise book in front of me. I saw what appeared to be a blueprint for a spider's web. 'These are the lines coming into Euston,' he said.

'"Algebra Book, Exercise 17 (a), Nos. 1–5",' I read from the detention book. 'That's what you're supposed to be doing. "Flipping blotting paper at the ceiling" is Mr Parker's allegation.'

'Oh no, look,' said Grayson. 'This is absolutely your only chance of having the lines into Euston explained to you by an expert. Now, this is the down main—' '"Much have I travelled in the you-know-what",' bawled Bolton, dashing Grayson out of the way. 'Now come on, Gilbert. Be a sport.'

'Come back,' I said, 'when you know it.'

At my elbow appeared Davis G. F. E., grinning with cosy satisfaction. Davis positively enjoyed any feature of school life, and detention was equally included. 'Write out Exercise 27 three times,' he said briskly. 'I've brought my own paper.' He opened a small case and extracted a sheaf of foolscap. It was, I noticed, already headed 'Detention. 12.6.47.' Beneath the foolscap were two neat parcels, wrapped in greaseproof paper, and a medicine bottle filled with ink.

'Detention is a sort of picnic to you,' I said, amazed.

Davis smiled, clearly finding nothing odd in the comparison. 'I'll have my tea first,' he said, and at once had one of his parcels unwrapped and was nibbling cosily at a cheese sandwich.

'All this time,' said Grayson, 'you've been missing a most marvellous discourse on the railway system at Euston – which, let me tell you, is known intimately to very few.'

A cricket ball crashed against the wire guard on the window. 'You're out!' 'I'm not!' 'He's out, isn't he, Windy?' 'Don't be a damned silly blasted fool!' 'Oh Jesus Criminy! I'm not playing then!' 'Well, fart off, Gingerballs!' I thought of the official view of cricket at The Vale, fostered by Mr Juniper and Mr Diamond, as a pastime marked by great courtesy, vast readiness to acclaim the achievements of the other side. It was slow to take root among the boarders.

'Look, Gilbert,' bawled Bolton. '"Fe-alty!" "De-mes-ne!" It isn't fair! Nobody could be expected to remember words like those!'

'I hope this satisfies you,' came Musk's silky voice. 'Though I must say you were terribly unfair.' He thrust a sheet of paper into my hand.

'"The Dangers of Talking too Much",' I read. '1. If you are talking about a person he (or she) may hear and think you mean something nasty. You can lose a lot of friends like that. 2. If you are talking politics and saying how bad one government is, you can get arrested by the police for slander. 3. If you talk in class and the master hears you he usually gives you a detention. 4. If you talk a great deal in public you get known as a bore and people avoid you.'

I looked up, feeling irritably humble, and caught Rosie's bland eye. 'Thank you,' I said. 'It's all true,' he murmured, backing through the door.

Grayson closed in, a fervent look on his face. 'Or like stout Thing-ummy, when with something eyes,' Bolton was shouting at the back of the room. Sounds of a multiple scuffle – including noises that might have been the snapping of necks or legs – came from outside the win-dow. 'And now,' said Davis happily, making a neat pile of his grease-proof paper, 'to work.' I looked at the clock and noticed that, as always happened on detention evenings, someone, who should certainly have been among us, appeared to have glued the hands to the face.

7

The summer bloomed enormously, and at times I seemed to have found my way into some gently haughty English middle-class fantasy of correct fairweather living, with perfectly kitted small boys perform-ing the rites of cricket, and classes blinking over their books in the school yard. Mr Diamond went into shirt sleeves: and roared his apologies at any woman who appeared. You'd have thought from the bluff fuss he made that he'd stripped to the skin. 'It's the heat, dear lady, you understand,' he'd explain to Mrs Leach; and no one would have been surprised to find that he'd put the sun down for a slippering.

My noisy ease as a teacher increased daily. I might have been quite the master of my classes had I been able to control my instinct to tease. When things seemed to be going well between Rose-M and me, I would feed my exhilaration into the classroom. Little Woolley, for example, a boy for whom the inevitable adjectives seemed to be 'keen' and 'decent' – natural captain of Middle Four, just and firm and given to flushing at the smallest hint of rough dealing – filled me with delighted affection for . . . the way he was what he had to be. That was it; I felt a helpless fond amusement caused by their conformity to their own characters. Woolley was unable to avoid being judicious and truthful: so he said to me once, carefully, 'I think you're not *quite* so nice as you were last term.' I collapsed with joy at the pronounce-ment; and Woolley gazed at me sadly. He was perfectly capable of informing Mr Juniper himself that his qualities seemed to be in decline.

Woolley was not much amused by the other habits that prevented me from becoming a competent teacher. Perhaps it was because of some basic frivolity that I allowed myself to be overwhelmed by their desire for amusement. I would see the classroom situation head-ing towards a joke and would positively omit to change course. I would even do a little steering in that direction myself, anxious that they should achieve the enjoyment they'd promised themselves. I was also given to bursts of positively nonsensical rhetoric. 'Of all boys', I would cry, 'you are the most wretched in the world'; and they were thrilled, and sometimes actually cheered. 'Oh, I do think you should get on', said Woolley once, at such a moment.

Most afternoons were given to cricket: and I was not much better at taking that than I'd been at taking football. My mind would drift away from the bickering slowness with which a game developed. It was easy to absent myself for a whole over, to find I had no views at all about some sudden passionate allegation of l.b.w. or run out. There were always, in any game, boys who claimed to know the rules by heart. They would appeal to a point that sounded at once slyly plausible and inane. If *A* did this at the same time that *B* did that, then *C*'s wicket was forfeit: 'It happened last week, Gilbert, in the game at Lords!' What I really needed was to have the inner council of MCC in constant session on the edge of the pitch. My charges would climb on to the bus, on their way back to school, horribly inflamed.

When I could, I cut a game short so that we had time to walk back to The Vale. I shrank from what a couple of dozen small boys could do to a peaceful mid-afternoon bus. They turned it into a shrieking turmoil; other passengers would look stunned. Once as we surged forward on the pavement, the conductor took up a fighting position. 'You can get on,' he cried, sounding like some doomed general preparing for a famous defeat, 'but you'll keep your traps shut. This is a bus, not a blooming roundabout.' I smiled weakly at him: he muttered, 'Try to keep the little buggers quiet!' It was odd, and not unsatisfactory, to think for a moment of those expensively educated children as little buggers.

Curiously, though he'd made prep school teaching his profession, our new maths master Mr Coyle was very much of the bus conductor's opinion. In a dry, unexcited fashion, he cherished the precisions of elementary mathematics, and was always complaining of the boys' work in the manner of someone who sees hooligans trampling his trim lawns. 'One boy in a hundred,' he'd groan, 'has the tidy mind for it.' He seemed always to have a headache. 'I can't bear their *thin screeching* voices,' he told me once, his own voice trembling with something close to hatred.

A cornerstone of Mr Coyle's philosophy of teaching appeared to be his determination never to be required to take part in cubbing. 'It isn't safe for grown men,' he claimed. And it seemed that the danger he was concerned with was not the moral one of popular discussion. Coyle claimed to have known prep school teachers who, lured into being cubs and scouts, had ended up with hernias, irreparably fractured limbs, broken noses, and other kinds of maiming. Some had simply had massive heart attacks and perished in mid-salute.

Certainly the strain on the heart could be measured on any grand cubbing occasion throughout that hot summer. There was a ceremony in the school yard when the district commissioner came to pass on some message of invigoration and encouragement. At the centre of a three-sided gathering of cubs and scouts stood Mr Beesley, holding one of the most enormous flags I'd ever seen in the care of a single person. At his side, rigid in widebrimmed hat and shorts, stood Todd. A teacher largely of English, Todd was a man of rather fine-drawn opinions, with busy views on Italian painting of the early Renaissance; and I could never reconcile the finicky austerity of his features with the outmoded empirebuilder's garb that he sported every Wednesday, and the glimpse of square red knees it offered – not, one absurdly but firmly felt, the knees of a lover of art.

The district commissioner stood facing the two masters, a crumpled man, muttering into a small white moustache. At once boys began to faint. The first was borne off by Todd, the second by Mr Beesley; and thereafter the rescue squad expanded to include most of the male members of the staff, methodically stepping among the dwindling ranks of boys and bearing off the unconscious ones as, with an equal effect of method, they sank to the ground. The commissioner continued with his address, and seemed at the time and afterwards very far from abashed by the reaction to it: which, without undue self-deprecation, might have been taken as unfavourable.

I found it difficult to restrain an absurd feeling of quite savage rage when a class failed to understand my explanation of a new piece of mathematics. It happened that term with Upper Four and simultaneous equations. I'd prepared myself with great care: setting myself problems, and solving them, till I felt I'd positively invented the process. The trouble was, as always, that their questions sprang out of areas of doubt as to the commonsense of mathematics that I'd never conceived of. So the whole notion of equality, without which one must naturally be rather cynical about any equation, was not acceptable to many. They retreated to a point of human development where this idea of one thing being equal to another had actually to be discovered and demonstrated. They nibbled away at the simultaneous equation till all I had left was a mass of pre-mathematical debris. Someone accustomed to dealing with primitive tribes might have moved forward from this point. I simply lost my temper.

And suddenly, all their exercise books had become scandals of untidiness – of blots and ill-formed letters and figures. From the junior school they'd brought a mass of conventions as to setting-down, underlining: being rough over here, being neat over there. Mr Juniper had once said, with his eye on Mrs Leach, that ladies were too concerned with neatness. But I couldn't believe that the implication – that some kind of decent masculine raffishness might be aimed at – could possibly cover the grubby confusions that filled my own exercise books.

I consulted Peter Nicholas, who felt simply that matter was more important than manner. I was unconvinced. Surely tidiness was a convenience as well as a grace? Wasn't there a point at which its absence constituted a collapse of the power simply to communicate? Had my classes passed that point? It seemed horribly probable that they had. They would never recover, and would fail to pass Common Entrance. I should have ruined the lives of scores of boys, and dashed the socially absurd, yet humanly inevitable, hopes of their parents.

I wondered what teacher training would have to tell me about such problems. The news of the emergency scheme was gloomy. Colleges were concentrating on an intake of women, since the great need was for primary-school teachers. It seemed my faults must wait for correction.

There were, as it happened, problems that no training could have helped me to solve. One was created by the unusual hours kept by some local ladies, and their curious forgetfulness in the matter of curtains. After midmorning break, that summer term, I took Lower Four in one of the attic classrooms. I would arrive and begin my lesson somewhere about eleven o'clock. At ten past eleven, regular in her mysterious irregularity, a young woman in the flats opposite would begin to undress. Tiny teasing clouds of what I took to be silk and other subtle materials would form and vanish in the world framed by her bedroom window. There'd be elbows, there'd be . . . shoulder blades? I'd feel my eyes fairly crossing. Shame and excitement would work together to disrupt any teacherly qualities I'd managed to bring with me into the room. Such shame, such shame! Could there be any dereliction of duty worse than that of a teacher who, in order to glimpse remote and microscopic fragments of female body – doubtfully identifiable at best – should neglect his pupils? It was obvious that their parents did not pay the exacting fees demanded by The Vale so that I might use the school as a platform – a skulking-point – for . . . *voyeurism*. Lord, yes, that was the dreadful word for it! I'd become terrified then that the boys might discover the direction and so the cause of my distracted gaze, and might, all fourteen of them, swivel in their seats and gaze with me. It would be as if I'd actually added this disgraceful occupation to the timetable. 'What do we do with the decimal point . . . ?' I would falter. But she'd bend down, across there, and another cloud would sail across the room and vanish, and I would seem to see . . . oh my goodness . . . the base of a spine, was it?

I found myself saying to James: 'I have, you know – you must have noticed – got myself rather entangled with Miss Perkins. An absurdity, you'll have thought it.'

'My dear chap,' said James. He looked and sounded like someone who'd been waiting for ages for a companion to confess to – oh, a bad headache, a blister on his foot? 'We've noticed it—'

'We?'

'The whole town has been buzzing with the news . . . No, seriously. I've been a little worried now and then. I realized it couldn't be serious, but you really have a talent for making your own going difficult—'

'Oh yes. I turn the smallest distance between two points into a desert. There I am, crying out for water—'

'Telling your friends to go on and save themselves – you'll just drop where you are and wait for death!'

Good Lord, how sensible James was! How sensible, suddenly, I was myself.

'If you can't enjoy the girl, in an ordinary straightforward fashion, then look elsewhere. That's my advice. But I think you must be cured by now, surely. I mean—'

I didn't want to hear what James meant. The very word 'cure' seemed to create the condition itself. I'd been lying under that mass of rock and suddenly it was papier mâché. 'She is . . . rather affected,' I said.

'Well, I should have thought so. I should have said that. The way she refers to quite famous dancers by their Christian names—'

'The family way of life—' I said.

'Incredible! All that twittering and pirouetting! And really, you know, when you think of the kind of man she fancies—'

'Eh?'

'Struggling across your desert you may not have noticed it – well, the fact is I've seen her off and on with – Oh, an airman or two. A sporty fellow in one of those very low motorcars.'

'Good Lord, yes – that sort of man! Rugger-players!'

That was not an exact term, as James and I used it. We'd both been indescribably fatuous on the rugger field: both had rebelled against the game as an almost politically charged instrument of the process by which the grammar school sought to make 'gentlemen' of us. The war had been, among other things, a war to end rugby football – or at least to halt it in its tracks.

'Possibly,' said James: not to be rushed off his feet even by revulsion.

'Several men, you say?' The vessel of my growing detachment grazed its bottom on a rock, there. But it sailed on. 'Believes in several strings to her—'

'Bow,' said James. After a pause he gave the startled laugh that always followed his discovery that a joke lay within his reach. 'Several strings to her beaux!' Then, anxiously: 'You see my – er – ? B-e-a-u-x, beaux.'

'Yes, yes,' I said. I didn't want anything to spoil the classic simplicity of this discussion, and the purgative consequences I felt it would have. 'The fact is she is . . . a little fickle!'

'My dear chap! Very fickle. Fecklessly fickle, you could say.'

I left him as soon as possible. When James made one of his occasional rediscoveries of the possibility of humorous statement, all hope of consequential conversation had to be abandoned. 'A spoilt child, and you're well free of her,' he said in parting. 'Better – ah – to be free *of* her than free *with* her and – ' 'You've helped me a lot,' I said hastily.

I felt, for a day or so after that conversation, a sense of having been truly cured, brought to my senses. Of course, of course! She was not of my kind, and wasn't even faithful.

But I must reflect how rash it would be to enter too jubilantly into this new inheritance of mine, of plain common sense and – hmm – emotional stability. I must consider what followed from my need to hear the truth in another's voice. I should have been able to tell myself these things, firmly and finally. Oh yes, I must be wary. Stability was not quite my forte, as it were; and I must grow accustomed to it bit by bit.

But then . . . hadn't I, in that talk with James, been tasting the vulgar joy of abusing Rose-M? Hadn't I delighted in James's plain speaking? And was I not now ashamed of my delight? And was I not now delighting in my shame? It was a baffling vista of emotions, each cannibalizing the one it followed.

But I *was* free, surely? Oh yes, I was free, and glad of it. Natural enough, in such circumstances, that gladness should have the taste of disappointment – and even grief . . .

At times, as the days passed, this careful pattern of thinking fell apart, and I knew that I was trying, cruelly pleased, to imagine the puzzlement she must feel at my silence. She would certainly be puzzled . . . and hurt. I shrank from the discovery that I was enjoying this notion, of her perplexity and pain.

Then I ran into her in our High Street. She was softly reproachful . . . took my arm, talked brightly: then, as we passed the spot where we'd exchanged our first kiss, eight months before, said: 'October 18th'. I was shaken by the implications of so accurate a memory.

Much later we lay among the legs of that shining piano and I was talking about teaching. 'I really want, you see,' I was saying, 'to get into the State schools and . . . Well, I think it may be possible to decide what to teach in the secondary modern school simply by looking at the way ordinary people live and deciding what's wrong with it. Do you see?' I was enormously earnest. Rose-M looked down at my hand, which, when the subject of teaching was curiously broached, had arrived at a point on her thigh. Engrossed in my clumsy ideas about the secondary modern school, I'd foreborne to send further messages to this hand, which lay stranded on that warm whiteness. I think in any case it had already arrived at an area beyond the reach of any instructions I could give to it or any other organ. Aware of the direction of Rose-M's gaze, I stared in my turn at that impotent hand.

'Next weekend,' she reminded me, with curious emphasis, 'we shall be in Brighton with The Under Thirties . . .'

8

The sea slapped over the wall at Ovingdean Gap. We'd been picnicking, after wandering through the town and along the front. Brighton was new to me; I'd never seen so many bow windows, so many little balconies – scraps of black lace on the narrow white throats of the houses. It was a town in which the buildings were dandies. They drew themselves on the air like a series of stylish strokes of wit. Altogether Brighton seemed to be the world of The Vale turned elegantly frivolous . . . And now, the picnic debris rounded up, we were to visit the Pavilion.

Rose-M said: 'I have a headache. I think I'd like to rest. We can go later?'

Then, when I stared at her owlishly: 'You wouldn't let me find my way back to the boarding house alone? You wouldn't be so ungallant?'

I made what seemed our incredible apologies to the rest of the party – and we walked away arm-in-arm. I avoided James's eye. Rose-M said: 'You needn't treat me so like an invalid. It's not a *bad* headache . . .'

No one was in the entrance hall of the boarding house. No one was on the stairs. 'I think I'll lie down,' said Rose-M: and then astonished me by standing on tiptoe, instead, and kissing me with a lingering softness beyond my experience. She drew me into her room.

I was at a loss: like a man who, having wished for nothing all his life but to play Hamlet, steps on to the stage and is only then struck by the thought that he ought to have learned his lines. I had no idea beyond that of positively picking Rose-M up. It was an action less easily performed than I'd imagined: lurching was involved, and enough of my mind remained to appreciate that it shouldn't have been. But now, having her in my anxious grasp, I wondered what to do next. I could connect no imaginable sequel of such an action with the exact décor and general possibilities offered by this boarding house bedroom. Picking up a girl in one's arms, one ought to be able to proceed to a stream, to be crossed, or a horse, to be mounted. Something of that sort. I could only stand there, feeling at once idiotic and pointlessly bold. Oh such audacity of intention, inside me, and so little idea how it might be expressed! At last it struck me that I must have been moved to this awkward action by the deeply buried aim of laying Rose-M on one of the beds. I did this; but in doing it, managed to strike her head on the brass ball at one corner. 'My goodness,' I gulped. Rose-M sighed.

A dark fog was descending over my actions. I groped for some idea of what I was doing, and intended to do. Meanwhile, I stretched myself awkwardly over Rose-M's body and caught her face between my hands: at the same moment being sharply disturbed by the thought that the bedroom door was unlocked. There was nothing to prevent the landlady from entering. I was already aware that as to the sounds being made in the room, I was no reliable witness. As I was uncertain about what I was doing, so I was curiously unable to use the sense of hearing. For all I knew, we were breathing so hoarsely that the landlady might at any moment rush upstairs, believing that fire had broken out or that the upper floor was filled with panting burglars. As these ideas began to work on me, I heard Rose-M say, with what seemed a cool softness of utterance: 'Darling – the door!' I slipped from the bed and crossed the room and pushed home the bolt.

And now such confusion! There were so many mechanical difficulties of which my reading of literature had proffered no warning. It was horribly like what had happened in my first classrooms. It was, again, that problem of writing straight across a blackboard! I took it to be of fairly central importance that I should remove Rose-M's drawers. But I was not absolutely certain of this – and the activity itself, when I came to it, proved to have unmanageable overtones. A part of my mind played worriedly with the idea that this direct assault on Rose-M's drawers might seem a fairly intolerable display of sheer rudeness. So I plucked at them, wormed them down by slow fractions of an inch, as if leaving room for a disavowal of the action, should this seem advisable. Her voice came, gently: 'Let me take them right off, dear! They're so tight!' They were off, at once, and fluttered over the edge of the bed.

It was the very core of wickedness, then, that I'd reached at last, at the age of twenty-six. Alas, such inefficiency had taken over in every sensual department! To my difficulty of hearing, of being sure what I heard, was added a very great decline of vision. I could not see Rose-M at all, and certainly had no power to focus her legs, her thighs. Dreams and fantasies of lovemaking had included at their very heart the idea of looking, of long and leisured looking. One would feast the eyes. Given at last the opportunity to turn fantasy into fact, I subjected my eyes to complete famine. In my embarrassment and bewilderment, I could not even see her face.

I then, in some dizziness of activity, partly undressed myself. The unseemly overtones here were worse than when I'd engaged in my would-be noncommittal struggle with Rose-M's drawers. Such an unwelcome suggestion of quite other places and purposes! Such a dispiriting reminder of the inelegance of underpants! Such an impression of the grotesque loneliness of socks! Then, out of all this confusion, and some sense of chilliness, I began to butt away at poor Rose-M, as if to the besiegement of her eager portals I bore a veritable battering-ram—

Which now . . . Her hands were upon me, and I wanted to giggle. The virginal shock spread through my whole being. So it was true! . . . Cold her fingers, sharp her nails! She took me and placed me—

There I thrust with the misery of a man, in very truth, out of his depth. The shallow useless fluster went on for a moment or so. I heard her cries – strange sounds, breathless pleadings . . . Then I fell out, and lay there, in that very worried confusion of sensations at the heart of which, somewhere, lay also Rose-M. She said: 'Oh Edward!' I could not doubt that it was an unimpressed adjudication. But my feeling of appalling failure was accompanied by one of great relief. It was done. It was over. I'd certainly not passed the exam, and it wouldn't be nice when the results came out; but, for the moment, it was over. We dressed; Rose-M asked me to wait downstairs while she tidied herself; then, arm in arm, we went out into the streets.

We walked gently, silently, as if, fragile ourselves, we were walking on a world as frail as an eggshell. By now, queerly enough, I was in a state of some complacency. I wasn't even quite sure that I had failed, after all. I had nothing to compare it with. It wasn't so much that I thought lovemaking ought to be so free of achievement as this had been; it was rather that I had no measure at all of the negative nature of our encounter. There was even, deep inside me, a little swaggering . . .

But largely, still, the sense of convalescence. Or of having escaped from the worst effects of some alarming accident. I sat in a tearoom opposite my fellow-survivor and drank a recuperative cup. 'Oh Edward!' she repeated several times. I was inclined now to think this was an utterance expressive of some – yes, of some . . . unusual form of contentment – even if it was slightly melancholy and, in a most loving way, of course, exasperated.

I felt lapped by, as it were, her adoring displeasure . . .

Back home, I couldn't find the book I wanted, which I imagined being entitled: *Sex: The Hard Facts*. But I found something that would do. After half an hour with this very slim volume – it had been printed during wartime – I was aghast. It was as though I'd been stammering what I'd thought to be French, only to discover that it was German. No, it was worse than that. Literature, largely, had convinced me that I was a pretty emancipated young dog: this rather breathy brief manual made it clear that I had known nothing, and worse than nothing.

My inward face white, I wondered if Rose-M had thought I was . . . well, pulling her leg would hardly do as a phrase, in the context. But something of that sort, all the same.

How could she believe that a man of twenty-six would act as though—?

Or as if—?

I saw my plain, simple tombstone. 'DIED,' it said, 'OF SHAME'.

The morning after her ordeal by way of my ignorant gallantries, she'd sat beside me in the boarding house living-room, playing with a kaleidoscope. Her manner had been edgy, teasing, oddly bright. I'd felt her nails again, now digging into my soul.

'Look,' she kept crying, handing me the kaleidoscope, but jogging it so that I could never hope to see what she'd admired. 'Oh, you're clumsy!' she cried.

While part of me observed this mysterious behaviour of hers with wary interest, a larger part, given less to observation than to the enjoyment of emotion, was busy with the feeling that we were now committed to each other. That curious encounter had been a sort of wedding ceremony. I said: 'One day, perhaps we shall pick up the skill of handing a kaleidoscope from one to the other'.

'One day?' said Rose-M.

'One day,' I said, feeling a nervous happiness.

'Oh look!' said Rose-M, and took the kaleidoscope from her eye. But this time she let it fall heavily into my lap. 'One day!' she said again, with what I took to be a sort of tenderly wry twist of the lip . . .

9

Back at The Vale, our days were in the grip of high summer and the events that belonged to that quite desperate season. Parts of the school were hushed, as scholastic emergencies arose; boys famous for their promise were known to be receiving their ultimate polish in the billiard room, a corner of Mr Juniper's study, the large cupboard known as the library. There was a rash of lecturers from outside, including a celebrated parent or two, a highflying Old Boy. One of the latter gave an illustrated talk on a region of Africa: the illustrations consisting of his disappearing at intervals into a room off the hall and re-emerging in tropical garb – headdresses, gowns, outrageously brilliant shirts, and a variety of exotic footwear. At times he brandished a spear or flourished a wicked-looking arrow. He loaded his ankles with bells intended to attract a lion. Mr Diamond found it necessary to forbid a certain quality of applause that greeted the early stages of this performance. In one of the lecturer's absences, he leapt on to a table, crashed his huge hands together, and, in a roaring whisper, intended to spare feelings as yet another costume was struggled with, declared: 'This is not a pierrot show, y'know . . . We are not on the pier at Southend. Jenkins, Jameson, whatever your name is – do you think you're on the pier at Southend?' Several boys whose names began with J hastily disclaimed any such illusion. The rest of the lecture was received with a nervous bubbling of enthusiasm and disbelief. The lecturer certainly had a mild English boniness of feature and deportment that made his disguises seem a series of gaudy impertinences at his own oddly willing expense.

There was a staff meeting which gave Mr Juniper an opportunity, of a kind he was always seeking, to throw doubt on modern approaches to education. As he read through a list of fourth- and fifth-formers, we were invited to call out, simultaneously, our verdict on each boy in terms of a scale from A to E. The agreement was astonishing, though I wondered if this was not a branch of extra-sensory perception rather than an exercise of cool judgment. Mr Juniper said: 'Why did they ever have to invent intelligence tests and IQs?' 'Indeed, sir,' said Mr Diamond. 'Give me the instincts of a sound schoolmaster, any time.' The sound schoolmasters round the table looked enormously pleased.

I thought, then, not for the first time, what a kindly staffroom it was. Such considerateness, as from man to man! I rarely heard voices raised; there was little if any disparagement of absent colleagues. Yet for all this, there was a massive unkindness of opinion as to the world that lay outside the pale of private education. Fatheads, clowns, brash malcontents, involuntary comics – such were the general mass of people, as seen by men as amiable as Harrod Parker. And even when it was a matter of dismissing the philosophy of a person of distinction who happened to be an enemy of social exclusiveness – even then, objections were phrased as if the faults in question were forms of vulgarity, social gaffes. So H. G. Wells and Bernard Shaw were, so to speak, enormous offenders in respect of the use of intellectual knives and forks and fingerbowls. It was *napery* again. Harrod Parker spoke especially of Wells with withering disdain. Mr Raisin referred to 'that jackanapes,' Bernard Shaw.

There was some xenophobia, too. In private, the term 'Anglo-Saxon' was used to explain the superiority of one boy over another. 'I was watching little Ashton-Baynes in the nets today,' Mr Diamond would say. 'It's good to see a thoroughly Anglo-Saxon young cricketer shaping up like that.' Mr Diamond was convinced that ability at cricket was a straightforward product of racial purity. Your little Central European was distinguishable by his elderly stoop and his innate helplessness when it came to wielding bat or ball. 'It's in the blood,' Mr Diamond would say, with a matter-of-fact assurance that suggested he had himself inspected, under a microscope, the precise item in that fluid from which skill at cricket sprang.

To Mr Diamond, in the teeth of much evidence provided by The Vale, any sharp order of intelligence – certainly anything that could be described as cleverness – was a mark of the alien. There were always boys who became irate symbols to him – and when he wished to speak of this foreign energy of mind, the name that came to his lips, time and time again, was that of a boy called Weinberger. Weinberger's qualifications as a symbol lay partly in the accident of his having very weak sight; he peered at the world through the thickest of glasses. He had also an elderly, disenchanted face, and did not conceal his gruff amusement at much in The Vale's daily existence. He once confessed to me that he had difficulty in ranking members of the staff in order of oddity. 'I mean, is Mr Diamond funnier than Mr Hollow? Mr Hollow is slightly more absurd in the way he speaks, but I think Mr Diamond is more ridiculous in the way he moves about the place. Have you noticed how he always takes those enormous strides? It makes him look so busy, but just think about this. How busy *is* Mr Diamond, really? What would you say?' 'Oh come! I'm not a person to put that question to!' 'You're being loyal, aren't you? I'm collecting absurdities; and being loyal is absurd. Why can't you tell me what you think?' I'd look up sometimes, in the midst of The Vale's affairs, and see those thick lenses turned upon us all sceptically, and Weinberger's head set at a scornful angle. He was among some boys who, one morning break, hung about at the edge of a discussion between Harrod Parker, Mr Capper and myself. We were talking about the teaching of Geography, and agreeing that Geography might make less sense that it should if it were altogether divorced from History. As I walked away to my next class I found Weinberger at my elbow. 'Look here,' he muttered, impatiently. 'What has Henry VIII got to do with the North Pole?'

The end-of-term exams made me uneasy, guilty. Not now because I feared they'd expose my ineffectiveness as a teacher. What I shrank from was the way a classroom on these occasions was filled with awed silence. It seemed such a flimsy confidence trick to practise on children. How could it hush even such boys as Lightfoot ii, Dennis, Hazard? I was ashamed of them, rather, for being hushed.

Invigilating Upper Four's Geography exam, I paused by Hazard's desk. I clasped my hands in front of me in one of the most ridiculous of schoolmasterly poses; I cleared my throat, in Mr Diamond's much-satirized fashion. On any other day, Hazard would have made wicked capital out of such actions. With rapid squeaking vagueness he'd have hinted at reasons for the placing of my hands ('Sorry, sir! Oh sorry, *sorry*!'); he'd have brought a lesson to a shrieking halt with his commiserations in respect of that cough, and with the madrigal of howls and sly whispers he and Dennis would have made out of them. Now he did nothing, said nothing: did not even look up. Only his pen squeaked.

I took advantage of this rare security and read his work over his shoulder. He had finished answering Question No 6, which itself consisted of a large number of snap questions. The last of these inquired: 'Where and what is the Port of London?' 'The Port of London' – Hazard had chanced his arm – 'is a port. It is in London.' I laughed, and he looked up briefly, haplessly.

It was a reversal of the natural order – or disorder – of things that gave me no satisfaction whatever.

The junior school sports were the earliest of the end-of-term galas. By then we could have done with a little of the cloud that had totally covered that now-incredible February. I was very nearly taken ill – this resulting from a combination of the great heat and Mrs Headstone.

Massive manipulations were a feature of the junior sports. I had not before understood the lack of scruple that underlay the conduct of a good junior school by its teachers. Certain boys must be jockeyed into winning positions for the sake of their morale – or indeed for their blue eyes or some other charming quality. Others, for the good of their characters, or for some special defect, must be excluded from triumph of any kind. The ladies of the junior school were like illusionists as they convinced their audience of victories or defeats – sometimes in the face of the plainest visual evidence. No one – not even the most quarrelsome parent – was given an opportunity for complaint. All was most beautifully contrived. Said Miss Seakins, as the last officially favoured boy marched off, blushing, with his prize: 'It has been a thoroughly satisfactory afternoon.'

I was amused, but my amusement was a little impaired by a growing sense of sickness. The afternoon had been very hot indeed. It was at the last moment, all prizes awarded, most boys safely surrendered to their parents or to nannies, that I ran into Headstone's mother.

Headstone was a quarrelsome, sorely egotistic child in Upper Three. He was deeply detested by virtually everyone. Very simply he set out to make as many people as possible as unhappy as possible. So he promoted quarrels, carried sad news and transmitted hostile opinions. He was horridly excited by any outbreak of enmity between any persons whatever. He fairly battened on occasions of punishment or disgrace. An unlikeable, dark-natured child . . . Ugh! everyone said. Ugh! – Headstone!

And now, suddenly, here was his mother, announcing herself. Her own face dark, angry, sulky. What did I make of Bernard? No, no, I was not to be polite. She could see I was trying to be polite about him. Miss Seakins had been so dreadfully polite. Mrs Headstone wished me to understand that she couldn't bear the child herself. 'I can't like him at all. Such a nasty child. At times – you will hardly believe it – but perhaps you will . . . at times I want to kill him. Now,' she said, 'this is my point. This is what I want to get from you. Miss Seakins won't say. I must know. Mr Headstone and I must know. Why is the boy so unpopular? Oh, I know, I know! Don't be polite. He is so dreadfully unpopular. We can feel it! We know it! You see, Mr Headstone and I have such a very large circle of friends. Tell me, please tell me. Your true opinion. Why do people dislike Bernard so much? It causes Mr Headstone and me such distress. We ourselves . . .'

My head was reeling. My sickness had become very acute and urgent. Her angry, egotistic eyes: the very hard line of her mouth, a hardness punched home by bright lipstick.

'Tell me, do. Tell me. Frankly. Mr Headstone and I would give anything to know why two such popular people . . .'

I was going to be actually sick.

'You need not be polite. Miss Seakins . . .'

Her angry, obsessive eye.

'Please,' I mumbled. 'I can't . . . must go . . .'

Her face swam, a puzzle of revolving hard mouth and angry eyes, and I ran and ran until I reached the darkest corner behind the pavilion, and there was very sick . . .

IO

My tendency to malaise, during those weeks of weather so bright that the most ordinary brickwork seemed suddenly beautiful, full of subtleties of colour – my queasiness and fatigue were partly an effect of very great uncertainty in respect of Rose-M.

It wasn't any longer that I doubted the outcome of our relationship. We must be married. All my largely literary sophistication had given way before a feeling that . . . oh, even ineptly to have made love was to be committed to each other. It was, surely, a clinching intimacy. Under my fast-fading sense of purely technical shame, I drew from the memory of it a profound and awestruck tenderness. It was altogether as if there had been some kind of physical fusion between us. Everywhere I heard her voice, her charming laughter: I could feel her fingers laced in mine. I looked searchingly into the narrow bright world of her face.

I was not able to enjoy these pleasures in reality. Rose-M had become curiously difficult of access. Notes came now and then: she was busy with end-of-term exams, trials, performances. 'I am dancing well, at last. They say I have a future!' This frustration of my desire to see her was one of the reasons for my uncertainty. There were clearly dispositions to be made: arrangements, agreements – simple introductions. I must break the news of her official existence to my own family. And as the weather grew more intensely bright, and the streets full of summery girls—

Oh! So many of the women who filled the streets of that suburb, or looked out of its windows, were so beautiful! It was, for a citizen of the outer suburbs like myself, disturbingly like being promoted from the world of the supporting film to the world of the main feature. As I plodded to school in the morning, this modest young usher with his ancient briefcase, I was in fact seething with infamous inclinations – filled with a thousand formless desires. Such a general sheen of shapely legs, such a universal bright inviting red of lips, everywhere such curves of cheek – and, altogether, such a pervasive idea of so many potential caresses . . . There they went, on their tittering womanly heels – inflamingly coloured among the blacks and browns of the men. I would lower my head and trudge on, like someone compelled to use the summer sea as a common thoroughfare.

There were times when I thought that I could easily fall in love with a lamppost.

Soon, soon, when all these ends of terms were over and done with, then we'd come together and take the worldly steps that had to be taken. Whatever they were . . .

'Well, now,' said Mr Beesley. 'That projected visit of ours to the Phoenix . . .'

It was the best part of the school year since my colleague had laid the foundations for this expedition: but I knew by now with what profound caution he conducted all his affairs. On any group of excited, noisy boys he had an extraordinarily calming effect, simply because he would not be panicked out of his invariable attitude to all events: which was to take them item by item, layer by layer, inspecting and smoothing, until he had them perfectly pacified. Watching Mr Beesley faced with any of The Vale's common occasions of disorder, I was reminded of my father's way with an umbrella he'd just brought in, wet and rumpled, from the rain. He'd shake the thing, and then take it fold by fold, stretching and calming each fold, until the blowsy umbrella of a few minutes before had become a buttoned-up slimness, a black rapier. So it was with Mr Beesley and the boys: he was much in demand as a buttoner-up of dishevelled behaviour.

And so, too, with our evening out at the repertory cinema. All possible impediments removed over the months since the invitation: Mrs Beesley's convenience perfectly consulted and established: he now fixed a date. It was, I understood, to be good-natured Mr Beesley's way of officially acknowledging my existence as his colleague.

We ate wholesomely at a local restaurant. Mrs Beesley turned out to be even more opposed than her husband to rashness and speed. During the meal she pleasantly refused more than conditional agreement to anything Mr Beesley proposed. And he beamed as she did so. 'One knows indeed,' as he told me happily, 'that to every question there are more possible answers than any single human head can discover.' Mrs Beesley's modest human head nodded assent to this, with the smallest touch of reserve, and her hand was laid briefly on his.

I noted that, and thought tenderly of Rose-M.

Then we were sitting in the best seats in the Phoenix . . .

It was one of those tragic French films that I see, looking back, gave me a paradoxically comfortable pleasure. Or perhaps it was that, at this time, the faces of Jean Gabin, Michel Simon, Raimu, Fernandel, were faces to which one attached a pleasure that derived from admiration: and also from a vicarious sense, given by so much association with their images, of being oneself a Frenchman, riding a bicycle through a suburb of Paris, working in a French factory or driving a French train, lying on a bed with, preferably, Arletty and grunting out the monosyllables of a doomed passion in between puffs at the latest in an endless series of cigarettes. As the final, heartbreaking image filled the screen, followed by that splendid word 'FIN', we all sighed with a grieved satisfaction. 'One's withers are wrung, and how expertly and sensitively,' said Mr Beesley, paying great attention to the business of restoring his wife to the shelter of her overcoat. 'A nice, sad evening,' I said, and we stepped out into the moonlit street.

Two figures were crossing the road ahead of us. A man and a girl. He bent down, she stretched up, and they kissed. How like Rose-M she was, I thought, idly. How like the athletics required in our own case, when a kiss was to be exchanged.

Then I saw that it *was* Rose-M. She tucked an arm tighter into his, and they drifted on to the further pavement.

The moonlight broke the scene into cold silver squares. They stepped into brightness, they were swallowed up at once by a darkness that half-hid their movement round a corner. They were gone.

'Oh God!' I cried.

'Well,' said Mr Beesley, too sweet a man to allow the most outrageous ejaculation from a companion to go unabsorbed by his general hospitality of mind. 'One's feelings after some films tend to be . . . exacerbated, I suppose, is the word. And not films alone, one must allow. One remembers one's very powerful reactions to one's first *Hamlet*, say – and of course one's very first *Lear* . . .'

We were outside the tube station. Mr and Mrs Beesley were extending courteous hands. I seemed to touch them, I seemed to say, 'Oh thank you.' Then I was running. The moon was declaring, coldly, beautifully, that this was the commonest of human scenes. It had always been so. Betrayal was the essential human principle. I struck the walls as I passed with numb fists. I exclaimed aloud, and cardboard passers-by turned their one-dimensional heads as I ran.

It is only by hindsight that I observe how close my agony was to the suffering witnessed that evening, with the cultivated appreciation of discriminating filmgoers, by Mr and Mrs Beesley and myself, on the screen at the Phoenix.

I had not noticed before how full the newspapers were of advertisements in which women were pictured, in their underwear. Everywhere there was evil, smoky erotic evil – and everyone had known it but me. There was some trace of the poison in the mildest human act, the gentlest human face. Ah, for a while there were no gentle faces! Even my little pupils were products of acts of passion, behind which lay dark histories of sexual provocation and treachery. All love grew out of the weeping ruins of other loves . . .

After days of horror, during which the ordinary business of life seemed to occur soundlessly, numbly, I made myself ring Rose-M.

'Oh, where have you been?' she cried, gaily. 'Among other things,' I said, every word a bruise, 'I have been to the Phoenix . . . that was on Wednesday, and you were there, too, and not alone, and as we came out I was just behind you and you were crossing the road and—'

There was a long silence. Then Rose-M said, in a small slow voice: 'I had wanted to talk to you – I had wanted to tell you—'

I said: 'Oh well – it was bad luck,' and found that I had hung up.

Her letter, waiting when I got home the following evening, said: 'I am punished for my cowardice. I had been trying to summon up the courage to tell you. Well, now it must be said like this, and I'm sorry, because I know how you will be hurt. The fact is that I am engaged. I am going to marry Tony Baker, of whom you have heard. Please let us meet and let me explain things as best I can. Please do that, for my sake as much as for yours.'

I was not generous enough for this. I composed letter after letter – cries of rage, some of them: laconically chilly, others. In the end I wrote: 'Congratulations. Don't bother about a meeting. I will work it out for myself.'

I shut myself up, then, with the terrible chorus of voices in my head: the angry ones, the self-pitying ones, the genuinely heart-broken ones, and those that spoke of my plight in disgracefully dramatic terms – rather pleased that I was so interestingly hurt. These last voices, I had enough detachment to note, were in the line of those that had spoken to me when I was a little boy, who'd badly hurt a leg, and was cheered by the thought of the attention he'd attract with his bandage and his limp . . .

Detachment grew, bit by bit. I saw that the weekend at Brighton had been the twilight of our love, not the new dawn I'd thought it. She had wanted at least, out of her guilt, to give me some physical consolation. But her guilt was surely unnecessary. It was I who was guilty. It was I who had allowed myself the hurtful luxury of my second thoughts, my attempts at withdrawal, my long recoils and silences: my failure ever to be part of her family: my complete failure even to introduce her to my own.

She was wholly innocent. For a moment, thinking this, I hated her for having been so cool, so judicious, so carefully secret. The hatred fed itself on the thought of its being Tony Baker she was going to marry. Of course, the intrepid airman – the gallant, drinking, dancing Tony Baker, who would be on such easy terms with Rose-M's mother, would not hesitate to take lunch with her father – I heard them chuckling, man to man, and Mr Perkins saying: 'We couldn't ask for a more acceptable son-in-law.' Tony Baker, who would never bring his elbow down on the keyboard of that shining piano . . .

Never again – in the lee of that piano! Never again – those soft thighs, bright eyes . . .

Peter Nicholas said: 'You seem rather distant of late. Do you think it's quite the best mood in which to face the senior sports?'

II

I clung to events, solid and dependable events, as to a series of lifebuoys. And the senior school sports was among them: an occasion marked by a prodigious display of bad temper from Mr Diamond and Mr Hollow, combined.

When they put their angers together, they could do astonishing things. So it was as this typical Vale occasion came to a close. There'd been a brilliance of parents: immense joviality as favoured athletes reaped expected rewards, immense jocularity as favoured non-athletes performed with expected feebleness. Masters, decoratively blazered, smiled over their stop-watches, starting pistols, record papers. I noticed Todd, surrounded by boys and parents. Todd, a perfectly professional schoolmaster, from a family of such professionals, had an attitude to the boys that fascinated me. It was teasingly friendly: he would pick on some weakness in a boy and turn it into a joke. I was often surprised by the trait that he chose for such ritual merriment. With Tudor, the little musician, for instance, it was a habit of losing fountain pens. I thought the small cellist had many pleasant oddities of personality. I liked his fantastic shyness: I liked the odd mixture of shame and pride that he displayed whenever there was talk of his musical gifts. A capacity for losing fountain pens, if he had it, was a prosaic element in a character so subtly and touchingly comic. But always it was some such – I thought, dull – characteristic that Todd fastened on, and polished into a joke: in some queer way, needing to lay hold of a boy by such a process. He had, like several of my colleagues, a deep wish to be popular, to be surrounded – as he was that sports day – by boys drawn to him by his conventional teases. I had noticed a darkening of his face, sometimes, when a boy left him for another master.

The sports field was enfolded in the greatest possible atmosphere of charm, and of a curious, inbred facetiousness – yes, that was Todd's quality! – that was a mark of all The Vale's ritual activities.

Then, suddenly, the last race had been run, the awards had been presented by an amazingly distinguished parent: colourful mothers and long-legged sisters were beginning to drift away: and Mr Diamond and Mr Hollow had become angry, together.

It was, I suppose, simply the anger they felt because they wanted the day to be packed up, so that, among other consequences, they could themselves get away. They knew that boys, and even parents, if left to themselves, were able to extend an occasion endlessly. So they charged into action, most dramatically nipping in the bud any inclination in any quarter to drift or dally. 'Now off home! Off you go! Double up! Out and home!' Mr Diamond began to roar, clapping his hands and striding from group to group, taking in a parent or two, or a splendid sister, on the way. 'Butler, Buller, whatever you're called, let's see those legs moving, double, double, off home!' Mr Hollow was at it on another edge of the flock. 'Don't hang 'bout! Rabin, t'ke th't h'dle back to pavil'n! Don't arg', boy!' Mr Diamond darting to his aid. 'Come on, boy! Rubin, Robin, what's your name, pick up the hurdle and take it over to the pavilion and then off home! What's that? Supposed to leave hurdles there? Nonsense!' 'Hur' up, boy!' Baffled and horrified boys carrying hurdles, tapes, jumping posts in the wrong directions, and being pursued by masters who'd given orders that they were to be taken elsewhere altogether, or left where they were for the groundsman to dispose of. Mr Diamond and Mr Hollow together now, driving the bulk of the boys with amazing cries towards the gates. Boys going other ways, in response to Mr Diamond's or Mr Hollow's own orders, being angrily rounded up and herded with the rest. An appalled groundsman rushing here and there to prevent boys from helplessly carrying hurdles, tapes and so forth out of the ground . . .

Peter Nicholas and I stood watching. 'They can't have any nerves, you know,' I said, aghast. 'How else could they endure their own uproar.'

'What bothers me,' said Peter, 'is the thought that . . . perhaps they once did have nerves, like anyone else. I'm certain, you know, that I'd hate to lose my own, in quite that manner. Wouldn't you?'

Peter Nicholas was surprised when, late in the day, I told him I'd applied to be emergency-trained. 'You really want to go on and on . . .?' he murmured. 'Well . . . I can only say that the idea of thousands of irrational little boys stretching into the years ahead is rather frightening.' He shivered dramatically. 'Still . . .'

I ran into an old teacher of my own. His despondency we'd found exciting in the sixth form, where his candid disillusionment had become merged in our minds with his passion for the stories of Maupassant. To be melancholy, if not glum – and to garnish your sadness with irony – seemed then a mark of maturity. Now he said: 'To be a schoolmaster you have to be narrowminded – the reverse of sophisticated. We're a lot of nonentities really. The best men get out of it.'

I couldn't think that he was right about this. I'd surely known teachers who were neither drab nor naive. Yet about being trained, and committing myself to the profession, I felt woefully undecided, vague. I yearned towards other fates, other occupations. I even detected in myself an abominable feeling of being *too good* for teaching. Ugh!

The Vale held me tight, anyway. I'd grown, as it were, nervously fond of it: or of certain colleagues, certain boys. I liked, childishly, the sensation of being at home in the school. I was quite ridiculously proud of having been accepted in so foreign a world.

Still when I stepped on the stairs that led to the attic classrooms I'd hear the whisper running ahead of me: 'Gilbert! Gilbert's coming!' But that was now as oddly pleasant as it was professionally appalling. And in a recent prep a boy had called 'Gilbert!' and then looked guilty: whereupon Lightfoot ii had grinned at him, and then at me, and said: 'It's all right!' I concluded that he was reassuring us both.

I was called into Mr Juniper's presence. 'Ah – we said this was to be an experiment, didn't we? I think it's been a successful one. What do you say? Well, let's see – your salary as a probationer, I suppose that's the word, was £200 a year. From next term I think we ought to raise that to £300. Don't you?'

I offered no objection.

In the staff photo, posed in the sunny yard, my face looked much like those in other photos that hung along the corridors and that, among other things, enabled one to trace Mr Diamond backwards, to a bushy-haired youngster with unmistakable hands housed on his knees. The smile I wore seemed to be stamped into my face: a mark, I thought, of all the desperate good humour of that year . . .

Among the heroes of the swimming gala were my old enemies, Hazard and Dennis. Swimming was their only earnestness; I hardly recognized their set, solemn faces. Sleekly they darted through the green water, their hair turned to dark tight caps. I wished there were ways of making mathematics aquatic.

Grief sat with me still, for Rose-M. At times I was tormented by the thought of what she might say about me to her competent fiancé. I imagined the efficiency with which he'd be preparing for their marriage. I saw him sitting at ease in front of a heap of documents.

I saw him being terribly able in bed – in many beds . . .

But it seemed to me now that the astonishing feature of my relationship with Rose-M had lain in none of its commonplace disasters, but in the way such real tenderness had arisen from a few evenings spent together. So few, really. There'd been a time when she'd invited me to dinner and the table had been set with candles that wouldn't stay put in their holders. There'd been this touching grandeur of the candle-lit table, and the more touching failure to carry the stage-management through. We'd quarrelled about politics, or about remarks of mine that Rose-M had identified as being political (and so unsuitable for a meal with candles): and that had been followed by hours of murmuring and nuzzling . . .

Well, I understood now that I'd not begun to know how to be a lover, in the ultimate sense. But perhaps it hadn't all been frustration and illusion?

The final Running-over of the year was a full-dress affair, revolving round an immense recital of marks awarded, expectations fulfilled or exceeded, hopes villainously dashed. A speech was made by a public school headmaster – a young, brisk, sharp man: I wondered, looking from him to Mr Juniper, if I'd have been tolerated on the staff of The Vale by a younger head. Mr Juniper had a capacity for eccentric action that might be no quality of a new generation of private school men, more managing – altogether less agreeably odd. This afternoon, for example, he was as nervous as an actor about to play Hamlet – and had made time for his routine correction of my spine and general posture. 'Chest out!' he'd urged, moulding me into a shape so unnatural that I was afraid a boy would catch sight of me before I could decently abandon it.

Mr Diamond had received many gifts from grateful boys and parents: several boxes of cigarettes, a lighter, a dictionary ('Always jolly useful, you know!'), a bottle of wine. He had been excited into a state of quite alarming general friendliness. Some boys clearly found it difficult to believe that his hand might be descending between their shoulder blades for amiable purposes.

Peter Nicholas made as little as possible of his pleasure at escaping. But when I asked him to send me occasional news of the larger world, he looked at me keenly and shook his head.

'Deliberate self-imprisonment!' he said. 'Very odd!'